The
Answers Book

Detailed answers at layman's level
to 12 of the most asked questions on
creation/evolution

Ken Ham ● **Andrew Snelling** ● **Carl Wieland**

(with special thanks to Rev. Peter Gadsby who contributed Part B of
the answer on the 'gap' theory — modified from *Creation* magazine,
vol. 7, no. 4, June 1985, pp. 30–31).

Creation Science Foundation Ltd,
P.O. Box 302, Sunnybank,
Qld, 4109, Australia.

MASTER BOOKS

Master Books,
P.O. Box 1606, El Cajon, CA, 92022,
USA ● (619) 448 – 1121.

ISBN 0 949906 15 8

Published by
Creation Science Foundation Ltd,
P.O. Box 302,
Sunnybank, Qld. 4109,
Australia

CONTENTS

ABOUT THE AUTHORS

KEN HAM, B.App.Sc., Dip.Ed.

After completing a Bachelor's degree in Applied Science (Biology) and a Diploma of Education, Ken was a science teacher in Queensland public high

schools before committing himself full-time to the message of creation and the Gospel. A director and one of the co-founders of Creation Science Foundation of Australia, he currently holds a senior position with the Institute for Creation Research in California. An internationally renowned Christian feature film (*The Genesis Solution*) has been made around his delivery of one of his major messages. He is author of several books, including *The Lie: Evolution* and *The Genesis Solution*.

DR ANDREW SNELLING, B.Sc.(Hons), Ph.D.

Andrew completed a Bachelor of Science degree in Applied Geology with first-class honours at the University of New South Wales in Sydney, before commencing Doctor of Philosophy research studies in geology at the University of Sydney, on the Koongarra uranium deposits east of Darwin in the Northern Territory. Between studies and since, he worked for six years in the exploration and mining industries in Tasmania, New South Wales, Western Australia and the Northern Territory variously as a field, mine and research geologist.

Now full-time with Creation Science Foundation, Dr Snelling is still called upon as a geological consultant by Denison Australia Pty Ltd, and is involved in research with CSIRO (Commonwealth Scientific and Industrial Research Organisation), ANSTO (Australian Nuclear Science and Technology Organisation), and university scientists, and with a team of international scientists from the USA, Britain, Japan and Sweden. As a result of this research he is involved in writing a growing number of

scientific papers that are being published in international secular scientific journals. He is editor of *Ex Nihilo Technical Journal*, is a Director of Creation Science Foundation and its senior research scientist.

DR CARL WIELAND, M.B., B.S.

Carl graduated with Bachelor's degrees in Medicine and Surgery from the University of Adelaide in 1973. He worked in private medical practice in the Adelaide metropolitan area from 1974 until mid-1986, when he moved to Cairns. He was a foundation member and President of the Creation Science Association from its inception in Adelaide in 1977 until it merged with the Brisbane-based Creation Science Foundation Ltd. He served with the Foundation in the capacity of Advisory Board member, and is currently its Managing Director. He has lectured widely in the field of science, creation and biblical apologetics to lay, professional and academic audiences. Dr Wieland was for some years President of the Christian Medical Fellowship in South Australia. He was founding editor of the magazine *Ex Nihilo* (now the international magazine *Creation*) to which he is a frequent contributor.

PREFACE

IN the past few decades, there has been a tremendous upsurge in the numbers of scientifically trained people who believe that God's Word in Genesis reveals a totally true (though not exhaustive or detailed) outline of the origin and history of all things.

Not only that, but they believe that it is a vitally important foundational issue. Genesis gives us the true origin (and therefore ultimately the meaning) of not only most major biblical doctrines, but virtually all of reality — life, death, love, marriage, clothing, mankind, the earth, good and evil, language, the universe itself.

The truth of the 'good news' about Jesus Christ depends totally upon the truth of the 'bad news' about Adam's rebellion against his Maker. Because Adam's sin brought the curse of death and bloodshed upon a sinless, deathless world, God the Son shed His blood in death so that those who believe in Him would not die eternally. Evolutionary explanations, with their eons of senseless suffering and death before man, oppose the entire sweep and flow of Old Testament and New Testament cosmology.

'For since by man came death, by man also came the resurrection of the dead. For as in Adam all die, even so in Christ all shall be made alive' (1 Corinthians 15:21–22).

The 12 questions addressed in this book are the most common ones heard at meetings after people have been exposed to a broad, general creation science presentation, showing that there is in fact a great deal of evidence for biblical creation/Flood.

The spirit in which such questions are asked, of course, may vary from enthusiastic seeking for reasonable answers, to sarcasm of the 'betcha can't answer that' variety.

The answers given are not meant to be infallible or 'the last word'. Some questions have answers that are easier and more satisfying than others. If it were not so, the reader might well have cause to suspect that we just wrote a book of answers to the 12 easiest questions, rather than the 12 most common ones. No doubt, as research continues, further facts and observations will come to light that will cause some of the positions to need modification or a shift in emphasis — perhaps even a total overhaul. If anyone reading this should demand an absence of unsolved problems before even considering creation, that would seem unreasonable in light of the plethora of huge problems surrounding evolutionary explanations. The 'answers' and 'proofs' given to students a generation ago in support of evolution have virtually all been discarded and replaced, or severely modified, without any diminishing in enthusiasm for this belief. Doubtless the same will ultimately happen to those now current. That is the nature of science, particularly origins-science, no matter what the philosophical framework within which it is conducted.

The reader should also remember that vast sums of taxpayers' money are spent on evolution-oriented research into origins, as against paltry numbers of both researchers and dollars operating within a creationist framework. In spite of this, the case for creation has become remarkably strong, and the remaining difficulties are now able to be seen as research challenges more than insuperable hurdles.

The two creationist organizations on separate continents, namely, Institute for Creation Research in San Diego, USA, and Creation Science Foundation in Brisbane, Australia, with which the authors are associated are also engaged in and supportive of such ongoing research efforts. This in itself refutes the common caricature that a creationist has no need for research, and simply goes to the Bible for glib answers.

The Bible is the unchanging, infallible Word of God (as authenticated by the living Word, Jesus Christ). Where it makes clear pronouncements (e.g. no death before Adam, Noah's Flood not local, etc.) we are totally committed to these by faith. It is the secondary theories and models which should be held lightly, as they do not have direct Scriptural authority. For instance, the Bible speaks of 'the waters above' the atmosphere. A model of a vast pre-Flood greenhouse vapour canopy neatly reconciles many biblical and scientific issues, and so is commonly held by creationists, including ourselves for the moment. However, no matter how attractive in other respects, a vapour canopy as such is not a direct teaching of Scripture.

The answers in this book certainly begin with the Bible as the basic framework within which to correlate and to understand those facts and observations relating to origins. The answers are meant to show that such a faith-position is not unreasonable, despite any residual difficulties. The authors maintain, of course, that it is far more reasonable and satisfying, both intellectually and spiritually, than the usual faith-position. That is, faith in a universe which consistently generates its own complexity (in violation of its own laws), faith in fossil links not found, in biological mechanisms never observed, and faith-belief in incredible transformations which are unobservable and unrepeatable by definition.

Our hope is that many Christians will be helped to be able to give a *'reason for the hope'* (1 Peter 3:15) and be better able to (gently and meekly) defend their faith. More than that, our prayer is that God will use these 'answers' to enable many to humbly accept God's sacrifice of His Son, Jesus Christ, as the price for their rebellion, the reconciliation between themselves and their Creator. And that in doing so, they may cross the line from eternal death to eternal life.

THE AUTHORS.

ANSWERS IN BRIEF

Just to whet your appetite, we thought we'd first give you the answers in summary:

QUESTION: 'What happened to the dinosaurs?'

BEFORE the Flood, dinosaurs and man lived together on our planet. Extinction of the great marine reptiles, along with the majority of all other types of sea creatures, would have been caused by the violent upheavals of the Flood, many being buried and preserved as fossils.

Two of each kind of land-dwelling dinosaur survived by being taken into the Ark. After the Flood they faced a radically different and more hostile world, and became extinct, along with countless other less spectacular creatures, some time after. There is some evidence that men knew about dinosaurs for a short time (perhaps several centuries after the Flood) before they finally became extinct. The descriptions of behemoth (Job 40:15) and leviathan (Job 41:1) quite possibly refer to some of the few post-Flood giant reptiles still in existence at that time. Job is thought to have lived before the time of Moses (i.e. before 1400 BC) but the writer of the Psalms (Psalm 74:14; 104:26) and the prophet Isaiah (Isaiah 27:1) also make mention of the great beast 'leviathan' and they are dated much later. Added to this is the obvious fact that not **every** square inch of this earth has yet been explored, and there may yet be some of these intriguing kinds of creatures alive on our planet.

QUESTION: 'What about continental drift? Have the continents really moved apart?'

MOST people today believe that earth scientists have proved that continental drift has occurred in the past, and still is occurring. What they are not told is that there are many well-qualified earth scientists who have much evidence contrary to the whole idea of continental drift as it is currently proposed. For example, the coastlines of the continents do not fit together neatly like a giant jigsaw puzzle — the much publicized apparent fitting together of Africa, South America, North America and Europe actually leaves out Central America altogether!

Furthermore, the 'fossil' magnetism (palaeomagnetism) of some rocks which is supposed to prove that the earth's magnetic field has reversed in the past, can be shown to be able to change of its own accord and so is not necessarily related to the earth's magnetic field after all. In any case, drilling into such 'fossil' magnetism-containing rocks on the ocean floor has shown that the actual 'fossil' magnetism in these rocks bears no resemblance to the interpretations that are supposed to explain how the continents were pushed apart. And without a viable mechanism to move the continents, it's no surprise that claims of having actually measured the moving of the continents using satellites can be shown to be premature.

The Bible does not mention continental drift. However, the Dodwell asteroid impact model can account for many of the geological and topographical features of the earth's surface which have been interpreted as indicating continental drift. Yet some creationists are still convinced that continental drift must have rapidly occurred by some mechanism(s), not now operative, at the close of the Flood or as a separate post-Flood catastrophe (e.g. when Genesis 10:25 says that in Peleg's day the earth was divided, meaning, in their view, continental drift rather than the division at Babel).

QUESTION: 'What about carbon–14 dating?'

THIS whole dating method is dependent upon knowing what the C^{14}/C^{12} ratio was at the time of the organism's death. The value used is based upon the **assumption** that the C^{14} in the atmosphere has long ago built up to 'steady state' — that is, the amount entering the atmosphere is in balance with the amount leaving (by decay). The **fact** is that modern measurements show that C^{14} is still building up rapidly and this would mean that the whole atmosphere is much less than approximately 30,000 years old. This would also have the effect of making C^{14} ages artificially 'older', especially the earlier dates. There are a number of other effects which would increase this tendency.

In addition, occasional 'anomalous' results, such as living creatures' having 'died' thousands of years ago, inspire caution about this method.

QUESTION: 'Were there really ice ages?'

THERE is good evidence for only one ice age, in the so-called Pleistocene epoch of the evolutionists' time-scale, just before man is presumed to have left written records. Evidence cited by evolutionists for earlier ice ages is open to other interpretations. Today's polar ice caps and alpine glaciers are the remains of the vast ice sheets that covered about a third of the globe at their greatest extent. The Ice Age must therefore have occurred soon after Noah's Flood.

Evolutionary geology, based on the uniformitarian (slow and gradual) belief, is at a loss to explain the evidence of the catastrophic arrival of the Ice Age — for instance, the 'snap freezing' of great hairy extinct elephants (or mammoths) in Alaska, Siberia and elsewhere. However, such catastrophism is readily explainable within the biblical framework of Noah's Flood and its after-effects. Whether or not the impact of an asteroid or an icy comet triggered the Ice Age, the collapse of the pre-Flood water vapour 'canopy' (the 'waters above') at the outset of the Flood year (the opening of the 'windows of heaven') would have produced a profound and permanent change in the earth's immediate post-Flood climate. Rapid cooling at the poles and warming at the equator would have induced excessive snowfalls and the build-up of the vast ice sheets, until after a few centuries conditions stabilized and the ice retreated. References to ice in the book of Job are consistent with that patriarch having lived at this time.

QUESTION: 'Why did God take six days?'

THERE has been much discussion in Christian circles concerning the meaning of the word 'day' in Genesis in reference to the six days of creation. However, looking at the meaning of the Hebrew word *yom* and the context in which it is used, plus other Scripture references, it is quite obvious that the days of creation in Genesis must be taken as literal solar days of approximately 24 hours in length. For instance, Exodus 20:11, which is the basis of the fourth commandment, tells us that God created everything in six days and rested for one, and that man was to copy that pattern. This, in fact, is where the seven-day week comes from. God didn't work for six million years and rest for one million years. How could He then tell us we should do the same? He worked for six days and rested for one, and this is the pattern which we copy today. There are also many other reasons why the days must be taken as ordinary days and why it is important to do so.

QUESTION: 'How did harmful things such as snakes' poisonous fangs come about, since they were not a part of the world before the Fall?'

THERE are differing viewpoints on this. Scripture overwhelmingly portrays a pre-Fall world with no violent death/struggle/bloodshed. Structures apparently designed for attack/defence are widespread. Most are marvels of engineering design. If one maintains that they all came about by degenerative mutations, this would appear to ignore the whole argument from design. (The word 'harmful' in relation to mutations refers to survival, not to the fact that a creature may have design information enabling it to harm another.)

The evidence for and against the argument that all such structures may have had a different function pre-Fall is discussed. Instances where such a change of function is clearly possible are described. Other possibilities are raised, including the obvious one that they were designed by God, either directly by alteration of DNA material after the Fall or through the unleashing of previously 'latent' genetic information. (The Bible makes it clear that God foreknew the Fall.) It is likely that some combination of the different possible suggestions was operative. The need to be careful not to argue outside of biblical boundaries is stressed, as well as the fact that Scripture does not give us adequate information on this subject to be dogmatic about mechanisms.

QUESTION: 'Noah's Flood — where did the waters go?'

THE water for Noah's Flood came from the release of great underground sources of water (the 'fountains of the great deep' which continued pouring forth for 150 days) and from the collapse of 'the waters above' (presumably a vast water vapour blanket or canopy above the atmosphere) giving the 40 days and nights of rain. Psalm 104 indicates that after the Flood the mountains were upthrust to their present positions with associated deepening of the ocean basins, which now hold the waters of the Flood.

These waters would not have been enough to cover today's highest mountains. Genesis indicates no rain or rainbows before the Flood, which is consistent with the absence of high mountains that are important to the triggering of rainfall. Also, the absence of large temperature differences between poles and equator under such a 'greenhouse blanket' of water vapour would mean an absence of the vast winds which are also necessary (now, but not before the Flood) for the rainfall cycle. Genesis describes how the earth before the Flood was watered by mists and/or springs and geysers.

QUESTION: 'How could all the human races come from Noah, his three sons and their wives?'

MODERN genetics shows that when a large, freely interbreeding group is suddenly broken into many smaller groups which from then on breed only among themselves (as the biblical description of the language dispersion at Babel would imply), different racial characteristics will arise very rapidly. It can be shown that one pair of middle-brown parents could produce all known shades of colour, from very white to very black, in ONE generation. The racial characteristics which exist today have not 'evolved', and generally speaking, are simply different combinations of pre-existing (created) genetic (hereditary) information. The environment plays a secondary role in favouring certain combinations over others.

QUESTION: 'What about the "gap" theory?'

THIS attempt to harmonize science and Scripture arose as belief in an old earth became prevalent. A time-gap is proposed between Genesis 1:1 and 1:2, during which the ancient original world was destroyed catastrophically as a judgment on

Lucifer's rebellion. The six days are then taken literally as the time involved in a re-creation.

The three main problems and inconsistencies of this theory come about because the long ages it seeks to incorporate are said to be represented by the successive layers of fossil-bearing rocks.

1. By placing this fossil record before Adam, gappists thus must place death and struggle before the Fall.
2. The catastrophe proposed to destroy the pre-Adamite world would have destroyed or reworked any pre-existing fossil record of long ages, thus eliminating the main reason for the theory in the first place.
3. The world-wide Flood of Noah, in spite of its scriptural prominence, is thus given an insignificant or non-existent role in accounting for geological evidence, in favour of a postulated catastrophe about which the Bible is silent.

There are other problems and inconsistencies, not the least of which is the fact that it is based on an unnatural and grammatically unsound interpretation being imposed on the text.

Being unable to satisfy the requirements of uniformitarian/evolutionary science in the slightest, it fails in its original intent to 'harmonize' this with the Bible.

QUESTION: 'Where did Cain get his wife?'

THE Bible teaches clearly that all human beings are descendants of Adam and Eve — thus there had to be inter-marriage between brother and sister. There would have been no risk of this causing harmful deformities in the offspring, because mutations (accidental changes in the hereditary information) need time to occur and accumulate in a population. Thus the first few generations would have inherited perfect or near-perfect genes, largely undamaged by mutations. In the pre-Flood world, harmful radiation from the sun and other cosmic sources was considerably more filtered than it is in the post-Flood world. Increased radiation and depletion of oxygen in the atmosphere (subsequent to the lowering of the atmospheric pressure) may have contributed greatly to man's rapid degeneration. With the passing of many centuries, many of these harmful, degenerative changes became added to the human race, so by the time of Moses it was absolutely necessary to have laws against incest, and these were given to mankind (Leviticus 18–20). Today there would be even more chance of deformity/disease in the offspring of such a union than in Moses' time. Because of the long life-spans, Adam and Eve's descendants may have been very numerous and widely dispersed before Cain even took a wife — that is, any inhabitants of the 'land of Nod' would have been descendants of Adam and Eve, who 'had many sons and daughters'.

QUESTION: 'How can light get to us from stars which are millions of light years away in a universe which the Bible claims is only thousands of years old?'

MEASUREMENTS made on the speed of light (denoted by the symbol c) as well as a number of related quantities, suggest that c may have been decreasing, tapering off to a seemingly constant value around 1960. This suggests that light was much faster in the past, and so there was enough time for light to get to us from the most distant object in only a few thousand years. This controversial possibility also has implications in a number of other areas, including the speed at which the radioactive elements used in dating procedures decay. Isotope ratios resulting from a higher past value of c would thus have been erroneously interpreted as giving ages up to billions of years.

There may be several other evidences for c decay, including published data which seem to indicate that atomic clocks have been slowing down over 26 years of observation. This suggests that c decay may be continuing at a very low level. This theory also gives rise to consistent explanations for many other phenomena.

Even if c decay in historical times can never be confirmed, it remains a fascinating possibility prior to that time. Thousands of years of light-travel time and radioactive decay would be erroneously interpreted as billions of years. One Russian professor of astrophysics, though an evolutionist, has independently proposed that a model of origins with c decaying (from a near-infinite beginning) fits the observations better than current theories.

QUESTION: 'How did kangaroos and other animals get to isolated places like Australia?'

IT is fully acknowledged that not all such problems have been fully solved, and some may never be.

Even in evolutionary belief, the ancestors of Australia's marsupials had to migrate between Australia and other continents. (Marsupials, and marsupial fossils, are found outside Australia.) Before the current popularity of the theory of continental drift, it was believed that during the Ice Age, lower sea level allowed migration on exposed land 'bridges'.

This seems to be the best explanation, though some creationists do hold to a form of post-Flood continental break-up. Individual animals don't have to be able to make the long journey; populations may shift geographically over many generations. A much moister world immediately post-Flood solves some of the apparent problems of food supply and crossing great wastelands.

The absence of the relevant fossils along migratory paths is to be expected, rather than a major problem. A tentative biological explanation (increased specialization with gene pool thinning and/or degenerative mutation) is offered as a possibility for the problem of survival of creatures with specialized diets and habits (their ancestors were not as specialized).

Some other related issues are addressed in the main article.

1

What happened to the dinosaurs?

THEIR bones were so big that when they were first discovered in 1677 by Dr Robert Plot they were thought to belong to a giant elephant. The first name given to them was *Scrotum humanum*. It was to be almost two centuries before the name 'dinosaur' came into existence.

In 1822 Mary Anne Mantell went for a walk along a country road in Sussex. According to tradition, she found a stone which glittered in the sunlight and took it home to show her fossil-collecting husband. Dr Mantell noticed that the stone contained a tooth similar to, but much larger than, that of modern reptiles. He concluded that it belonged to some extinct giant plant-eating reptile with teeth like an iguana's. In 1825 he named the owner of the tooth *Iguanodon* ('iguana tooth'). It was Dr Mantell who began to popularize the age of the reptiles. In 1841 Sir Richard Owen, the famous palaeontologist, coined the word 'dinosaur'. Technically, 'dinosaur' refers to those giant reptile-like creatures which lived on *land* rather than in the *water*. The word means 'terrible lizard'. In the minds of those who had been associated with the then recently discovered bones of a nine metre (30 feet) long monster with two metre (six feet) long jaws from the Lyme Regis quarries of England, the name was particularly appropriate.

BONES, EVOLUTION AND EXTINCTION

Nowadays, everyone has heard of dinosaurs. From kindergarten onwards, we see pictures of them, and as far as most people are concerned, they died out about 65 million years before man appeared on earth. This view of the dinosaurs is intimately associated with evolution, which is dogmatic about how life arose by

In 1822, Mary Anne Mantell found a stone glittering in the sunlight. It was this find which led to the popularizing of the age of reptiles.

chance, yet surprisingly vague about why creatures such as the dinosaurs died out. Citing every possible cause from massive attacks of diarrhoea, to meteorite bombardment, or drug addiction as new plant forms evolved, the theories of why the dinosaurs became extinct are often hilarious for their ingenuity.

A visit to any world-class museum will reveal abundant evidence that these dinosaurs really did exist. The bones and skeletons which have been dug out of the earth are obviously the remains of giant animals that once lived and died. Their skeletal remains have been preserved in the rocks. However, while bones testify to their existence, scientists have not always made accurate reconstruc-

tions. Everyone has heard about or seen pictures of *Brontosaurus* with its long neck, but not everyone knows 'Bronty' was a mistake! Scientists discovered that they had put the wrong fossil head on the wrong fossil body.[1] *Brontosaurus* never existed! For that reason, *Brontosaurus* simply doesn't get a mention in *The New Dinosaur Dictionary* by Donald F. Glut (Citadel Press, Secaucus, New Jersey, 1982).

It is important to realize that when scientists dig up a number of bones, they do not dig up an

animal with its flesh intact. Even if they found **all** the bones (and they often have only a few fragments) they still would have less than 40 per cent of the animal to tell them what it originally looked like. The bones do not tell the colour of the animal, nor what it ate for dinner. Even the presence of sharp teeth tells you only that it ripped its food, not what food it ripped. When reconstructing large dinosaurs from bony remains, scientists have had to make all kinds of assumptions. Likewise, any statements about what the dinosaurs did or where they lived are full of such guesses. Nevertheless, the evidence is overwhelming that the dinosaurs were indeed a large group of creatures that once roamed the earth, but now apparently no longer live on this planet.

So what did happen to the dinosaurs? According to the evolutionary theory, dinosaurs lived on the earth during the Mesozoic Era or the dinosaur age. This was between about 230 million and 65 million years ago on the evolutionary time-scale. Then at the end of the Cretaceous Period of the Mesozoic Era they died out. In August of 1983, Dr Alan Charig of the British Museum of Natural History,

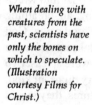

When dealing with creatures from the past, scientists have only the bones on which to speculate. (Illustration courtesy Films for Christ.)

London, and Dr Beverly Halstead of the Geology Department, Reading University, seriously challenged every evolutionary theory as to why the dinosaurs had become extinct or even when they died out.[2] Which serves to remind us that when it comes to dealing with past creatures, whether it be the history of dinosaurs or anything else, a scientist has only the bones upon which he can speculate. He doesn't have the past in his laboratory. He digs up the bones in the present. Any theory about what happened to the dinosaurs, based on bones alone, is merely a scientist's opinion. He was not an observer of the event, and he doesn't have the past to test his theory against. Thus such study is not even scientific in the normal sense. It is really his belief about the past, an attempt to explain the evidence which exists in the present. The only way anyone could be sure of what did happen in the past, would be through the testimony of any reliable witness who was there. And that is what the book of Genesis is. It is easy to test this claim. The accurate record of one who was there will always make the best sense of the evidence we have in the present.

DINOSAURS IN BIBLICAL HISTORY

Does the book of Genesis provide a practical basis for the scientist attempting to explain what happened to the dinosaurs? According to Genesis, land animals and man were made on the sixth day of the creation week (Genesis 1:24,25).[3,4] These days were ordinary solar days (Genesis 1 and Exodus 20:11), therefore, those dinosaurs which were land animals were created on the same day as the first man Adam. Both dinosaurs and man inhabited this planet at the same time.

And what did the dinosaurs do after the time of creation? Like all the other animals, they began to populate the earth. The Bible records that, as time went on, the earth became full of wickedness, so God determined He would send a world-wide flood to destroy 'all flesh that has the breath of life in it' (Genesis 6:17). He commanded a man named Noah to build a very large boat into which he would take his family and representatives of all land-dwelling, air-breathing animals. The Bible tells us clearly that when the time for the Flood came, God sent two of every kind of animal (and seven of some) to Noah to take up residence aboard the Ark (Genesis 7:2). Since the Bible is clear that there were at least two of every kind of land animal, this must have included two of every dinosaur kind. Many people think that because dinosaurs were such large creatures, they would never have fitted into the Ark. They do not realize that many of the dinosaurs were

not large at all; a few large dinosaurs have been given all the publicity, such as *Brachiosaurus, Tyrannosaurus, Diplodocus* and *Allosaurus*.

Many dinosaurs were quite small. For instance, *Struthiomimus* was only the size of an ostrich, and *Compsognathus* was no bigger than a rooster. Only a few dinosaurs grew to extremely large sizes, but even they were not as large as the largest animal in the world today, namely the blue whale. It is realistic to assume that God would have sent

Compsognathus — *no bigger than a chicken.*

young adults and not fully grown creatures. Since the animals that came off the boat were to be responsible for repopulating the earth, it is almost essential that only young adults which would later reach the prime of their reproductive life would be sent on board the Ark. Also, it must be remembered that Noah's Ark was extremely large. In their classic book, *The Genesis Flood*, Drs Henry Morris and John Whitcomb calculated the size of the Ark and the number of animals needed to represent all the kinds. Their calculations suggest that fewer than 75,000 individual animals would have been needed on Noah's Ark, and indicate that these animals could have fitted on only one floor of the Ark, since their average size would have been no bigger than a sheep. The Ark was more than large enough to carry representatives of every kind of air-breathing, land-dwelling animal.

So what happened to the dinosaurs? Genesis states that during the time of the

Illustration courtesy Brian Newton

Flood, water covered 'all the high hills that were under the whole heaven.' Any dinosaur not on board Noah's Ark which was a land-dwelling, air-breathing creature, would obviously have drowned. Many of them would have been buried rapidly and catastrophically in the Flood sediments and therefore preserved. Most of the dinosaur fossils we find around the earth today are probably all that remain of those killed at the time of Noah's Flood. The contorted shapes of these animals, the massive numbers of them in fossil graveyards, their wide distribution, and the presence of whole skeletons which show convincing evidence of being rapidly buried, all testify to massive flooding.[5]

Months after the Ark had settled on Mount Ararat, the animals came out to breed and repopulate the earth. Two by two, the dinosaurs, along with all other animals, left the landing place of the Ark and began to move over the earth's surface. But the world they came out to was a different world from the one they knew before Noah's Flood. It had been ravaged by watery violence. The water canopy which the Bible implies existed around the earth's atmosphere up to the time of Noah's Flood was gone. No longer was the world a 'greenhouse' covered in lush vegetation. The massive quantity of vegetable material which the larger creatures needed to consume as food was no longer available in such luxuriant abundance. The world was a much harsher place to live in. The environment before the Flood had been a favourable one. It had enabled many animals and plants to grow to enormous sizes. Most mammals reach their final size soon after becoming sexually mature. Reptiles, however, may keep growing almost

The environment before the Flood enabled animals and plants to grow to enormous sizes. (Illustration © Films for Christ.)

indefinitely after that time. In today's crocodile populations, for example, the very large specimens are also the very old ones. This is likely to have been the case for the occasional very huge dinosaur whose skeleton is found. The young, sexually mature adults ordered to go on board the Ark with Noah would have been nowhere near that size yet.

There had probably been a much greater land surface before the Flood. Plants had grown in great profusion and had provided food necessary for all the land creatures. But now the world was different; the canopy had been destroyed. The world had been denuded of vegetation which was now only newly regrowing. More radiation would be able to reach the surface of the earth, and even the atmospheric pressure in the absence of a canopy would be lower. Yes, the world was indeed a harder place to live in. The animals could no longer grow as well or live as long as they had in the pre-Flood environment.

The Bible records in Genesis 1:30 that when the first animals were created they were all vegetarians. Even the dinosaurs, lions and tigers were to eat only plants.

That's one reason why Adam would not have been frightened by *Tyrannosaurus rex*, for even that mighty beast, before the Fall, would have been a plant-eater. But Genesis states that after the Flood, God told Noah that from then on the animals would fear him, and from then on man could eat their meat (Genesis 9:1–17). Even for man the world had become a harsher place. In order for him to survive, the once easily obtained plant protein would now have to be supplemented by animal sources. Man was going into competition with the animals to survive.

One would therefore expect that both animals and man would find their survival ability tested to the utmost. It is a fact of history deducible from the fossil record, from the written history of man, and from experience over recent centuries that not all species of life on this planet have survived that competition. While we realize that vast numbers of marine species became extinct at the time of Noah's Flood, we need to remember that many plants and air-breathing, land-dwelling animals have become extinct only since the Flood, either due to man's action or competition with other species, or because of the harsher post-Flood environment. Many groups are still becoming extinct. Dinosaurs are certainly numbered among the groups that seem to no longer exist. Why then do people get so intrigued about dinosaurs, and have very little interest in the extinction of the fern *Cladophebius*? If it were not for their size and appeal as monsters, dinosaurs would have excited no more than passing interest. However, because of mankind's almost science-fiction fascination with the unusual, dinosaurs have become famous throughout the world. People are fascinated with the question: 'What really did happen to them?'

MAN AND DINOSAURS?

If the dinosaurs that accompanied Noah died out some time after the Flood, it would be expected that some evidence of co-habitation of dinosaurs with man in history could be discovered. Is there any evidence for this? Yes. Just as nearly every culture of the world has flood sto-

Compare the ancient American Indian drawing on the left to this recent reconstruction of the dinosaur Edmontosaurus *(white outline added for clarity). Illustration courtesy Films for Christ.*

*Just as nearly every culture has flood stories, many also have dragon legends.
Were these dragons really dinosaurs?*

ries similar to those in Genesis 6–9, many different cultures also have dragon legends.[6] It has been suggested that these are in fact encounters with creatures such as dinosaurs.

For example, in the film *The Great Dinosaur Mystery* (produced by Films for Christ) we find that a Sumerian story dating back to 3,000 BC tells of a hero named Gilgamesh who, when he went to fell cedars in a remote forest, encountered a huge vicious dragon which he slew, cutting its head off as a trophy. When Alexander the Great and his soldiers marched into India, they found that the Indians worshipped huge hissing reptiles that they kept in caves. China has always been renowned for its dragon stories, and dragons have always been prominent on Chinese pottery, embroidery and carvings. England has its story of St George who slew a dragon that lived in a cave.

But we are not just referring to stories dating back thousands of years, for even in the tenth century, an Irishman wrote of his encounter with what appears to have been a *Stegosaurus*. In the 1500s a European scientific book, *Historia Animalium*, listed several animals, which to us are dinosaurs, as still alive. A well-known naturalist of the time, Ulysses Aldrovandus, recorded an encounter between a peasant named Baptista and a dragon whose description fits that of the dinosaur *Tanystropheus*. The encounter was on May 13, 1572 near Bologna in Italy, and the peasant killed the dragon. So the evidence for the existence of dinosaurs during recorded human history is strong.

We also have the description of two beasts that could very well have been such great reptilian creatures still existing in Job's day (Job 40:15, 41:1–34). The text records that God was showing Job how great He was as Creator in causing him to observe some of the most powerful of the creatures He had made. In Job 40, verse 15, God tells Job to look at behemoth. In many commentaries, behemoth is said to be an elephant or a hippopotamus. However, this description is unlikely since behemoth is said to have had 'a tail like a cedar' (verse 17). Now if there is one thing an elephant's tiny tail is unlike, it is a cedar tree! The elephant is quickly eliminated as a possibility for this beast. In fact, after reading this passage in Job very carefully, one is hard put to find any living creature to fit the description. The closest that we know could be *Brachiosaurus* — one of the dinosaurs. Leviathan (Job 41:1) seems also to have been some form of fire-breathing dragon. For those who wonder about this, remember that the living bombardier beetle can shoot out super-heated gases in its own defence. Why not leviathan?

So what did happen to the dinosaurs? Those that did not go into Noah's Ark certainly would have drowned. Many of these were buried quickly and therefore preserved, and their bones have been found in recent times. Those that went in to the Ark with Noah survived, and after the Flood were able to breed and reproduce their offspring. However, due to the harsh conditions, shortage of food and so on, they have become extinct. It is hard to say categorically that any animal is extinct, since one can't scientifically prove an organism to be extinct. Geologists, the traditional declarers of extinction, have been severely embarrassed several times when after having declared animals to be extinct they have discovered them alive and well in environments the scientists merely hadn't looked at. It is neither possible nor feasible to have one person at every point on the earth's surface looking in every direction all at one time just to be 100 per cent

As late as the 1980s explorers and natives in Africa have reported sightings of dinosaur-like creatures.

sure that there are no dinosaurs and that therefore dinosaurs truly are extinct.

There have been reported sightings of dinosaurs even up to the present day.[7] In *Science Digest*, June, 1981 and as late as 1983 (*Science Frontiers*, No. 33), explorers and natives in Africa have reported sightings of dinosaur-like creatures. These have usually been confined to out-of-the-way places such as lakes in the middle of Congo jungles. But descriptions given certainly fit those of dinosaurs. It could even be true that the Loch Ness monster (if Nessie really exists) is a variety of *Plesiosaur* which still survives today. It certainly would be no embarrassment to a creationist if someone discovered a living *Tyrannosaurus rex* in a jungle. It wouldn't even be surprising if it happened to be a plant-eater! However, this would be a tremendous embarrassment to an evolutionist.

There is no real mystery surrounding the dinosaurs when one understands the events that have happened in the past. But our understanding of these events can-

In the grounds of the Crystal Palace in South London stand early concrete reconstructions of Iguanodon (illustration courtesy Brian Newton).

not be based on the mere speculations of people who are alive in the present. Unless they are based on the carefully recorded words of the Creator God who was there, none of us has a basis for any real interpretation of history or evidence at all.

FOOTNOTES

1. (Paul Taylor from Films for Christ supplied the following information.) For more than a hundred years, the *Brontosaurus* has been pictured incorrectly in every dinosaur book, textbook, advertisement, science fiction movie and museum in the world. Two researchers at Carnegie Institute have proved conclusively that the skeletons of the *Brontosaurus* in five major museums, including Carnegie, were given the wrong heads.

In 1979, David Berman and John McIntosh revealed to the Press the fact that the supposed authoritative description of the *Brontosaurus* given by the renowned palaeontologist Dr O. C. Marsh of Yale was based on a headless skeleton. In an article entitled 'Scientists Claim Brontosaurus Given Wrong Head' (Pittsburgh: Associated Press, October 10, 1979), Berman explained that Marsh 'actually used a head that was found three or four miles away from the skeleton. But no one knew. He never mentioned this in his article.' There was no evidence the skull had anything to do with the *Brontosaurus*. You can check this out in the publication, *Marsh's Dinosaurs* by John H. Ostrom and John S. McIntosh (New Haven, Connecticut: Yale University Press, 1966), p. 244. Proof positive of this rather serious error was unearthed as early as 1909, when Earl Douglas found a nearly perfect skeleton in Utah, complete with a much sleeker head. Although W. J. Holland published this important discovery in 1915, the find received no publicity or serious consideration, we presume for three main reasons: (1) because Marsh was considered the greater expert, (2) because of pressure from American Museum Director Henry F. Osborn, and (3) because, as Berman ruefully observed, 'old ideas die hard.'

The new head given to the *Brontosaurus* shows that the creature was actually a type of *Diplodocus*. Its skeletal characteristics are practically identical to those of the *Diplodocus*. The more delicate skull sports rather fragile-looking, pencil-like teeth. On this evidence, it has been suggested that the creature probably ate aquatic plants and tender grasses.

Even the whole area concerning classification of dinosaurs is quite complex. Palaeontologists are often confused as to where to assign certain fossils. For instance, many years ago dinosaur expert Dr O.C. Marsh invented a sauropod family named *Atlantosauridae*. Into this family he placed the *Brontosaurus*, *Apatosaurus*, and *Atlantosaurus*. Years later, A.S. Romer decided all three of these dinosaurs plus *Titanosaurus* were the same as *Apatosaurus*. In 1966, he changed his mind and reported *Apatosaurus* was different, but *Brontosaurus* and *Atlantosaurus* were the same. Later authors have felt that *Apatosaurus* and *Brontosaurus* are the same but that *Atlantosaurus* is different. The *Aepisaurus* and *Aegyptosaurus* may be the same as *Titanosaurus*.

There are a number of lessons to be learned from the case of the wrong-headed *Brontosaurus*. First, skepticism is always in order with regard to pronouncements of 'fact' by museums, science books, and experts. On further investigation, 'facts' all too often turn out to be only guesswork and theories based on preconceived ideas. Unfortunately, hard science can sometimes be found sharing museum halls with exhibits which propound the pet theories of resident curators or which exaggerate the validity of theories to satisfy the public's common desire for sensationalism. It took the prestigious Carnegie Institute more than 70 years to finally put the right head on their *Brontosaurus* skeleton, despite the fact that all the evidence was in the museum's own archives. One can imagine how slow a museum might be to change an exhibit which promotes theories held even more dear by many curators — such as the theory of evolution. Old ideas do, indeed, die hard. It is fortunate that intentional dishonesty and unintentional mistakes are not more common among palaeontologists anxious to outdo their rivals. It rarely comes to public attention. The *Brontosaurus* error and deception might never have come to light had it not been for the perseverance of researchers Berman and McIntosh.

Once the mistake was discovered, it was realized that the head belonged to a previously discovered dinosaur — *Apatosaurus*, and therefore did not deserve a new name. The body was that of a *Diplodocus*. It is not too difficult to realize that an animal with another animals' head **NEVER EXISTED**. The head had a different body and therefore it was not *Brontosaurus*. The body had a different head and therefore it was not **THE *BRONTOSAURUS*** everybody knows. Some museums, however, continue to display *Brontosaurus* with the wrong head!

2. 'All theories on the dinosaurs' extinction are now extinct.' *The Weekend Australian*, August 27-28, 1983, p.11 and *The Times*, London, August 25, 1983.

    These newspaper stories were reporting on the savage attack on all catastrophic dinosaur extinction theories made by Drs Alan Charig (Dinosaur Curator, British Museum (Natural History), London) and Beverly Halstead (Department of Geology and Zoology, Reading University) at a British Association meeting at Brighton, England in the last week of August, 1983. This attack was also reported in *New Scientist*, September 1, 1983, p. 606. Personal comments on the dinosaur extinction controversy by these two dinosaur authorities appear in *Nature*, vol. 304, August 4, 1983, p. 472 (Dr Charig) and in *New Scientist*, September 1, 1983, p. 633 (Dr Halstead).

3. Day 5a — the creation of all sea creatures (Genesis 1:20–23). This includes the entire spectrum from small fish to great sea monsters (v. 21) and includes plesiosaurs and ichthyosaurs.

4. Day 5b — the creation of all flying creatures (Genesis 1:20–22). This includes *Archaeopteryx* and flying reptiles, the pterodactyls.

5. For example, reptiles drowned in a flash flood 200 million years ago, according to the interpretation put upon the discovery of reptile fossils in the Lubnock Quarry, Texas. *The Weekend Australian*, November 26–27, 1983, p. 32.

6. Dragon legends appear in China, Japan, Australia, South America, India, Europe, England and in the Americas. 'Update', *Omega*, October, 1981, p. 32.

7. More than 40 people claimed to have seen plesiosaurs off the Victorian coast (Australia) over recent years. *Melbourne Sun*, February 6, 1980.

2

What about continental drift? Have the continents really moved apart?

THIRTY years ago most geologists were adamant that the information they had about the earth could only be explained by the idea that the continents were stationary. Only a handful of geologists promoted the notion that the continents had moved (continental drift), but those 'believers' were accused by the majority of indulging in pseudo-science fantasy. Today, that opinion has reversed. Continental drift is now the ruling theory (taught as fact), and those who dare question it are usually labelled as stubborn and ignorant.

What brought about such a dramatic about-turn? Between 1962 and 1968 four main lines of independent experiments and measurements gave rise to the 'remarkable' synthesis we çall 'plate tectonics':[1]

1. mapping of the topography of the sea floor using echo depth-sounders;
2. measuring the magnetic field above the sea-floor using magnetometers;
3. timing the north-south reversals of the earth's magnetic field using the magnetic 'memory' of rocks from the continents and their radiometric ages;
4. determining very accurately the location of earthquakes using the world-wide network of seismometers originally developed to detect nuclear blasts.

PLATE TECTONICS

The general tenets of 'plate tectonics' theory may be stated as follows.[2] The earth's surface crust consists of a mosaic of rigid plates, each moving relative to adjacent plates. Deformation occurs at the edges of the plates by three types of horizontal motion: extension (or rifting), slipping and compression. Sea-floor spreading occurs where two plates are moving away from each other horizontally

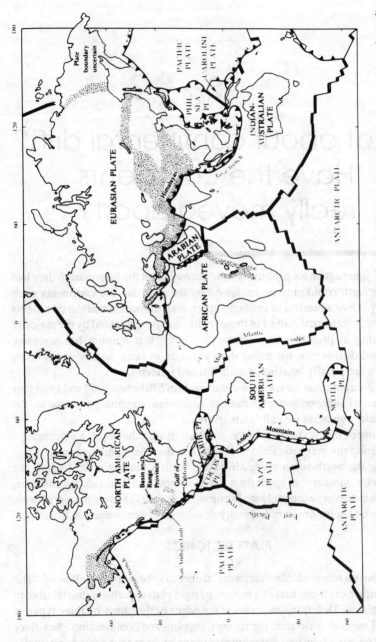

Simplified map showing how the earth's surface is divided into 'plates', some with continents and some without. 'Plate' boundaries are categorized according to interactions between the 'plate' boundaries. Spreading is believed to occur along the mid-ocean ridges (heavy lines), sliding along transform faults (thin lines — e.g. San Andreas Fault of California), and colliding where one 'plate' is being pushed under the other one along 'subduction zones' (barbed lines on overriding plate). Stippled areas within continents are regions of active deformation (e.g. earthquakes) away from 'plate' boundaries.

(e.g. the Mid-Atlantic Ridge and East Pacific Rise), with new molten material from the earth's mantle being added between them to form new oceanic crust. Transform faulting occurs where one plate is slipping horizontally past another (e.g. the San Andreas fault of California). Subduction occurs where two plates are colliding, with one plate being pushed under the other, producing compressional deformation (e.g. the Peru-Chile Trench and associated Andes Mountains of South America, and the Himalayan Mountains where the Indian plate collided with the Asian Plate). In keeping with their evolutionary-uniformitarian assumptions, geologists suppose that the plates move very slowly — about two to 18 centimetres per year. At this rate it would take 100 million years to form an ocean basin or mountain range.

Although most geologists today enthusiastically endorse this theory of drifting continents, there still remains a significant minority of very competent earth scientists who do not.[3, 4] Their objections are quite numerous, so only a few main objections will be summarized here.

FITTING OF CONTINENTS

The idea that the continents can be fitted together like a jigsaw puzzle to form a single super-continent is an old one, based on the interesting apparent 'fit' of the eastern 'bulge' of South America into the south-western 'concavity' of Africa. Recent investigators have used computers to try to fit the continents. But even one of the best reconstructions of how Africa, South America, Europe and North America once fitted together,[5] has areas of overlap between these continents, and Central America is omitted altogether! There are a number of ways to fit South America, Africa, India, Australia, and Antarctica, but if the theory is true only one can be correct. Some reconstructions have been shown to be geometrically feasible, but they

Can the continents really fit together like jigsaw pieces?

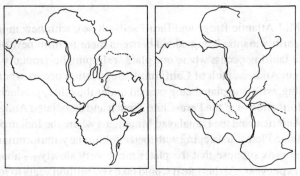

Two attempts at reconstructing the great southern supercontinent of Gondwanaland that is supposed to have broken up and drifted apart.

are impossible to explain by continental drift (e.g. rotation of eastern Australia to fit into eastern North America).[6]

SEA-FLOOR SPREADING

Evidence suggesting sea-floor spreading is claimed by many geologists to be the most compelling argument for plate tectonics. In the ocean basins, along mid-ocean ridges plates are thought to be diverging slowly and continuously with molten mantle-derived material being injected between the plates and cooling to form new oceanic crust. The youngest crust is claimed to be at the ridge crests with the rocks becoming progressively older away from the crests. At the time of cooling, some of the rocks' minerals acquire magnetism from the earth's magnetic field. Since the earth's magnetic field is supposed to have reversed numerous times in the past, during some 'epochs' the cooling oceanic crust should have been reversely mag-netized. Thus, if sea-floor spreading is continuous, the ocean floor should possess a magnetic 'tape recording' of reversals. It is claimed that a 'zebra stripe' pattern of linear magnetic anomalies parallel to the mid-ocean ridge crest has been recorded in some areas, while potassium-argon dating has been alleged to show older rocks farther from the ridge crest.

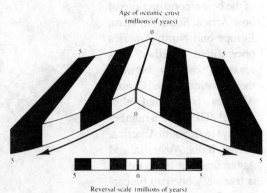

Researchers Vine and Mathews said the ocean crust was like a conveyor belt carrying the record of polarity reversals on both sides of the spreading sea-floor centre.

MAGNETIC STRIPES?

However, there are some very serious problems with this 'compelling' evidence. Rezanov[7] concluded *'that palaeomagnetic data are still so unreliable and contradictory that they cannot be used as evidence either for or against the hypothesis of the relative drift of continents or their parts.'* Asymmetry of magnetic stripes, not symmetry, is the normal occurrence.[8] Vine and Wilson,[9] among the leading early investigators, admitted *'as ever in the interpretation of magnetic anomalies, there is no unique solution, and the various parameters are so "flexible" that, having assumed normal and reverse stripes, the model can be fitted to any existing concept of the structure of oceanic ridges.'*

Furthermore, the magnetic bands may not form by reversals of the earth's magnetic field at all! Doell and Cox[10] state that *'the reversed magnetization of some rocks is now known to be due to a self-reversal mechanism'*. Jacobs[11] continues: *'Such results show that one must be cautious about interpreting all reversals as due to field reversal and the problem of deciding which reversed rocks indicate a reversal of the field may in some cases be extremely difficult.'* Thus the Meyerhoffs concluded *'the so-called magnetic anomalies are not what they are purported to be'*.[12]

But to settle the issue, Hall and Robinson[13] reported on recent deep crustal drilling in the North Atlantic Ocean. Drilling of magnetized rocks revealed *'the absence of the source for linear magnetic anomalies'*. They concluded, *'It is clear that the simple model of uniformly magnetized crustal blocks of alternating polarity does not represent reality'*. Why? Because the drilling revealed that down the holes *'a variation of magnetization intensity occurs on several scales from centimetres to tens of metres, and there are no consistent trends with depth'*. Furthermore, there is *'poor agreement between the sense of the effective magnetization in the drilled holes and the associated linear anomalies'*. In other words, the actual magnetism in the rocks on the sea floor bore no resemblance to the magnetism previously recorded from boats sailing across the ocean surface. Hall and Robinson were forced by the evidence to concede, *'It is apparent that crustal drilling has shown that the processes of generation and modification of oceanic crust are much more complex than originally thought'*.

LAND ANOMALIES

Meanwhile, the magnetic properties of rocks have also been measured on land, and it is now well established that there are large linear areas of rock within which are successive 'stripes' of reversed and normal magnetic 'polarity'. Humphreys[14] has recently reviewed the evidence for the validity of these 'fossil' magnetism studies and has found that fully half of all the 200,000 plus geological samples tested have a measurable magnetization whose direction ('polarity') is reversed with respect to earth's present magnetic field. He concluded that the variety, extent, continuity and consistency of the reversal data all strongly suggest that most of the data are valid, so that he had no option but to accept that reversals of the earth's magnetic field must have occurred.

The problem with the interpretation of these magnetic data is the presumed mechanism for operation of the earth's magnetic field and thus the presumed multi-million year time-scale for these reversals. The operational mechanism preferred by many geophysicists, the so-called dynamo hypothesis, has many problems associated with it which have been well documented.[15-18] The only viable alternative is the hypothesis that proposes freely decaying electric currents in the earth's core,[19-22] a mechanism that can account for the magnetic reversals recorded in the rocks having taken place in a matter of only days and years![23]

POTASSIUM-ARGON DATING

As to the 'successful' dating of the sea-floor magnetic anomalies, such a claim is doubtful. Wesson[24] says that potassium-argon dating, when correctly interpreted, shows no evidence of increasing age with distance from the ridge crest. Furthermore, others[25, 26] have found that the greater argon content (giving older apparent age) of the ocean-floor basalts on the flanks of the mid-ocean ridges can be explained easily by the greater depth and pressure at the time of solidification incorporating original magmatic argon (not derived by radioactive decay).

SUBDUCTION

A corollary to the idea of plate growth by sea-floor spreading is the notion that converging plates are destroyed below the deep ocean trenches, a process called subduction. The volcanic island arcs and coastal moun-
tain ranges associated with
the ocean trenches (e.g. the
Pacific 'ring of fire') are said
to result from remelting of the
subducted or underthrust
plate at a depth of up to
700km, while the deep and
high intensity earthquakes in
these same areas are assumed
to indicate movement and

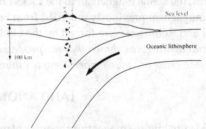

Sketch through a collision or 'subduction' zone. Many geologists believe that the 'oceanic lithosphere' (right) or 'plate' of ocean floor rocks, is being pushed under the continental 'plate' on the left.

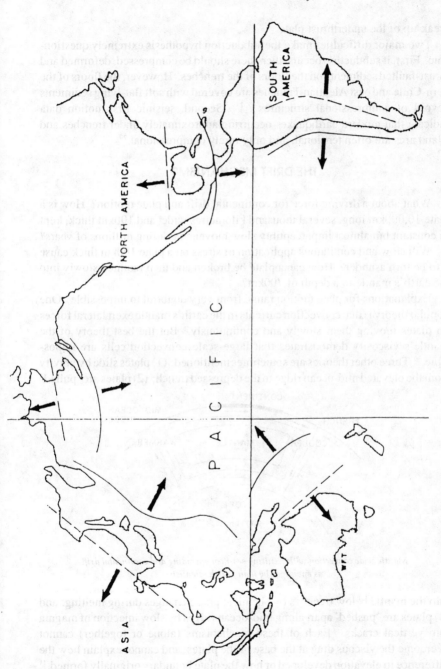

Plate tectonic theory predicts that earthquakes will be compressional along plate collision or 'subduction' zones. However, this sketch map shows that along many of these zones the forces producing earthquakes are tensional (that is, 'plates' are pulling apart)!

break-up of the underthrust plate.

Two major difficulties make the subduction hypothesis extremely questionable. First, if subduction occurs, then there should be compressed, deformed and thrust-faulted sediments on the floors of the trenches. However, the floors of the Peru-Chile and east Aleutian Trenches are covered with soft flat-lying sediments devoid of compressional structures.[27, 28] Second, seismic first-motion data indicate that modern earthquakes occurring approximately under trenches and island arcs are often tensional, and only rarely compressional.[29]

THE DRIFT MECHANISM?

What about a driving force for continental drift and plate motion? How is a plate 10,000km long, several thousand kilometres wide, and 100km thick, kept in constant but almost imperceptibly slow movement during millions of years?

Will slow and continuous application of stress on a plate 100km thick cause it to be torn asunder? How can a plate be broken and then rammed slowly into the earth's mantle to a depth of 700km?

Explanations for plate motion range from very doubtful to impossible. One popular theory is that convection currents in the earth's mantle exert lateral forces on plates moving them slowly and continuously. But the best theory of the mantle's viscosity demonstrates that large-scale convection cells are impossible.[30] Three other theories are sometimes mentioned: (1) plates slide by gravity from the elevated mid-ocean ridge to the depressed trench; (2) plates are 'pulled'

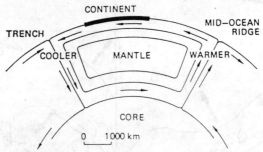

Mantle-wide convection with resulting sea-floor spreading and continental drift as envisaged by many earth scientists.

into the mantle below trenches by chemical phase changes during melting; and (3) plates are 'pushed' apart along mid-ocean ridges by slow injection of magma into vertical cracks. Each of these mechanisms (alone or together) cannot overcome the viscous drag at the base of the plates, and cannot explain how the difference in elevation developed or how the plate boundary originally formed.[31]

DRIFT MEASURED?

An article in *Scientific American*[32] seems to suggest, to the casual reader, that measurements have shown that the continents are drifting relative to each other. The authors closed their article with a map which summarized the results from two sets of observations — their own, between observatories on the Eurasian and North American plates (which are supposed to be moving apart along the Mid-Atlantic Ridge), and those from NASA, between the Pacific plate and the Eurasian and North American plates respectively, which are supposed to be coming together.

The most obviously impressive thing about these results is that in both groups of observations the direction of the apparent movement is that predicted by current theory (see Table 1). How impressive are the results otherwise?

Let us assume that the technique itself is inherently accurate and reliable, in spite of the fact that the accuracies claimed ('changes as small as a centimetre in relative positions of points on the earth'[33]) are mind-boggling over such distances. The reader may get the impression that the distance has actually been measured as varying by the amounts shown in each case, but this is not so. The results are given as a RATE. We are not told how this rate was obtained, how far the 'plate' really moved, and over what period of time.

OBSERVED (cm/yr)	PREDICTED (cm/yr)
(a) Carter-Wilson Observations	
+ 1.1	+ 1.7
+ 1.1	+ 1.9
(b) NASA Observations	
- 8.5	- 9.4
- 11.1	- 8.9
- 4.4	- 2.3
- 3.9	- 5.0
- 7.9	- 5.2
- 1.9	- 0.7*

Comparison of two sets of very-long-baseline interferometer observations with 'plate' motions predicted by computer models of 'drift'.

* This was between the Eurasian and North American 'plates'.

RANDOM FLUCTUATIONS!

The authors, Carter and Robertson, say in their opening paragraphs that the technique has been operational for more than a decade. But in January 1983, *Science News* reported that interferometry had been used to make measurements like this, looking for movement between plates, since 1979, and no one had yet detected any change![34] Carter and Robertson make no mention of this, nor do they attempt to give non-drift explanations for apparent changes in the baseline. They do, however, make a very telling admission:

'. . . *the baseline lengths are increasing at a rate of between one centimetre and two centimetres per year. On the other hand, the baseline lengths also exhibit equally large random fluctuations; hence from these data alone we would be reluctant to conclude that we had really measured plate motions.*'[35]

It appears that far more detail, and probably another decade or so of careful observation, would need to be reported before one could begin to reach satisfactory conclusions. It is currently just as valid to accept the four years or so of 'no change' reported to 1983 as to accept that drift has been 'actually measured'. However, the claim that continental drift has been measured will probably become the popular view from now on. Carter and Robertson themselves are commendably cautious:

'**Once** *we have accumulated enough observations to be sure the measurements of plate motions are accurate, the measurements* **will** *have great value as a check on plate-tectonic theory.*'[36] (Emphases added)

Unfortunately, they are less temperate in some earlier parts of the article:

'*Now we are beginning to measure . . . the baselines . . . getting longer by about a centimetre a year . . . we are watching geology happen.*'[37]

A CONTRARY RESULT

The most fascinating part of the whole article, however, is that two observatories on the North American continent (in Texas and Massachusetts, respectively) must, if one uses the same sort of approach to the data, be accepted as moving towards one another at a rate of one centimetre a year, even though they are supposed to be on the same **rigid** plate!

This makes nonsense of the Carter-Robertson claim '*it appears the VLBI* (very long baseline interferometry) *is indeed capturing plate tectonics in action*',[38] when this result is completely contrary to the current plate tectonic theory these 'measurements' are supposed to capture 'in action'. The current plate tectonic theory that was used in the computer modelling to predict what 'drift' values should be observed assumes 'the plates move at a constant rate and move rigidly, so that there is no motion within the plates.'[39]

By their own admission therefore, their measurement of contraction of the Texas-Massachusetts baseline within the North American plate disproves this assumption, throwing into doubt both the computer modelling, and the plate tectonic theory on which it was based.

NEW CLAIMS OF MEASURED DRIFT

New claims have been made at a 1989 conference that drift has actually been measured.[40]   David Smith of NASA reviewed the data collected since the late 1970s, via the space geodetic techniques of laser ranging to satellites and very ¹ong baseline interferometry (VLBI), and claimed that these measurements are confirming the geological predictions for motions between the major tectonic 'plates'.

However, these results are only from the continuation of the same NASA measurement program as that reported in *Scientific American* and *Science News*, the latter stating in 1983 that no one had yet detected any movements! Now Smith is claiming movements have been measured, but again he only reports the results as a RATE (e.g. 15mm/yr across the Mid-Atlantic Ridge, 170mm/yr across the East Pacific Rise, and 28mm/yr across the San Andreas Fault). But how far has the 'plates' really moved, and over what period of time? We are not told. Smith only says that overall agreement with models of plate motion based on geological data of the past 30 million years is very good, but how much have the evolutionary 'models' of geological data and time influenced the rate interpretations? We still have cause to be sceptical of such claims of measured drift, but await fuller documentation in the scientific literature.

Geologists usually explain folded strata such as these as being caused by mountain-building during 'plate collisions'.

A BIBLICAL PERSPECTIVE

If the continents have drifted in the past, then it is not yet clear from measurements that they are still drifting today. This is important to a biblical view of geology, not because the Bible speaks directly for or against continental drift, but because in the biblical post-Flood framework, if the continents (with their loads of Flood-deposited, fossil-bearing strata) separated to their present positions (e.g. at the time of the Tower of Babel, suggested by some because Genesis 10:25 says *'the earth was divided'* in the days of Peleg), the relatively short time involved would lead to enormous difficulties in accounting for the heat energy necessarily dissipated against friction — not to mention the earth movements and destruction at the earth's surface that would result from such rapid continent-wide motion. However, in the Dodwell asteroid impact model for the triggering of the Flood catastrophe, supported by seemingly impeccable astronomical data,[41,42] the existence of a crust which has been cracked into several 'plates' is no surprise. Nor is the evidence for increased volcanic and earthquake activity at the boundaries of those plates. Indeed, it would be a great surprise, in view of the inferred temperature differences between the earth's interior and exterior, among other physical factors, if there was absolutely no relative movement between plates once they had been formed by cracking of a previously unified crust (the breaking up of the 'fountains of the great deep'?).

Furthermore, the Flood model for the development of many of the earth's crustal strata can account for the magnetic 'stripes' in some layers that appear to record past countless reversals of the earth's magnetic field. If we apply the Barnes mechanism for generation of the earth's magnetic field, which is superior to the so-called 'dynamo' hypothesis, then the earth's magnetic field could well have flipped many times during and soon after the Flood.[43]

The mechanism for retreat of the Flood waters is also associated with tectonics. Psalm 104:6–7 describes the abating of the waters which had stood above the mountains. The eighth verse properly translated says, *'The mountains rose up; the valleys sank down,'* implying that vertical earth movements were the dominant tectonic forces operating at the close of the Flood, in contrast to dominant horizontal forces postulated in much of modern continental drift theory. It is significant therefore that the *'mountains of Ararat'* (Genesis 8:4), the resting place of the Ark after the 150th day of the Flood, are in a tectonically active region at what is believed to be the junction of three crustal plates.[44]

A metre or two of measured movement today is no issue, but if that movement, for several plates, is consistently in the direction predicted by theoretical models of plate tectonics, it appears to constitute powerful evidence for these. If such evidence does exist, and does stand the test of time, then the Dodwell model may probably be the most fruitful area to explore to explain initial rapid drifting of 'plates' during the Flood as they overcame the viscous drag of the earth's mantle for a short time due to the enormous catastrophic forces at work, followed by a slowing down to present rates. Such continental separation could potentially solve some other apparent geological enigmas — for instance, the amazing similarities of sedimentary layers in the north-eastern United States to those in Britain, but the absence of those same layers in the intervening North Atlantic ocean basin; the similarities in the geology of parts of Australia with South Africa, India and Antarctica, etc. However, as we have seen, to date the evidence from these measurements does not require any such reassessment. It should be noted that some are turning to the Dodwell model as an explanation for continental drift as a post-Flood catastrophe, occurring for example, in the days of Peleg.[45]

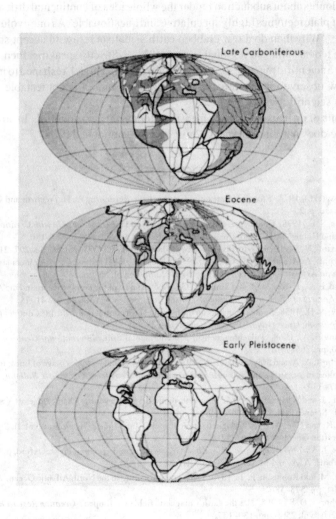

Wegener's reconstruction of the distribution of the continents during the periods indicated. Africa is placed in its present-day position to serve as a standard of reference. The more heavily shaded areas (mainly on the continents) represent shallow seas. (From A. Wegener, Die Entstehung der Kontinente und Ozeane, *1915).*

IN CONCLUSION

The absence of sufficient mechanism(s) for plate motion, the uncertainty regarding sea-floor palaeomagnetism and the existence of sea-floor spreading, and the doubts about subduction render the whole idea of continental drift and the theory of plate tectonics highly speculative and questionable. As one evolutionist has said: 'Why then do a few crabbed earth scientists refuse to accept some or all of the tenets of the "new global tectonics"? . . . Strictly speaking, then, we do not have a scientific hypothesis, but rather a pragmatic model, reshaped to include each new observation . . . obviously, this kind of model is not testable in any rigorous scientific sense.'[46]

Claims of drift actually being measured today are also doubtful. In any case, the Bible does not directly speak for or against continental drift.

FOOTNOTES

1. Cox, A. (Ed.), 1973. *Plate Tectonics and Geomagnetic Reversals*, W. H. Freeman and Co., San Francisco, p. 2.
2. Nevins, S. E., 1978. Continental drift, plate tectonics, and the Bible. In: *Up with Creation!*, Gish D. T. and Rohrer, D. H. (eds), Creation-Life Publishers, San Diego, pp. 173–180.
3. Beloussov, V. V., 1979. Why do I not accept plate tectonics? *EOS*, vol. 60, pp. 207–211.
4. Meyerhoff, A. A. and Meyerhoff, H. A., 1972. 'The new global tectonics': major inconsistencies. *American Association of Petroleum Geologists Bulletin*, vol. 56, pp. 269–336.
5. Bullard, E. C., Everett, J. E. and Smith, A. G., 1965. The fit of the continents around the Atlantic. *Royal Society of London Philosophical Transactions*, series A, vol. 258, pp. 41–75.
6. Voisey, A. H., 1958. Some comments on the hypothesis of continental drift. In: *Continental Drift, a Symposium*, University of Tasmania, pp. 162–171.
7. Rezanov, I. A., 1968. Palaeomagnetism and continental drift. *International Geology Review*, vol. 10, pp. 765–776.
8. Meyerhoff, A. A. and Meyerhoff, H. A., 1972. 'The new global tectonics': age of linear magnetic anomalies of ocean basins. *American Association of Petroleum Geologists Bulletin*, vol. 56, pp. 337–359.
9. Vine, F. J. and Wilson, J. T., 1965. Magnetic anomalies over a young oceanic ridge off Vancouver Island. Science, vol. 150, pp. 485–489.
10. Doell, R. and Cox, A., 1967. Magnetization of rocks. In: *Mining Geophysics*, vol. II, Society of Exploration Geophysicists, p. 452.
11. Jacobs, J. A., 1967. *The Earth's Core and Geomagnetism*, Pergamon Press, Oxford, p. 106.
12. Meyerhoff, A. A. and Meyerhoff, H. A., Ref. 8.
13. Hall, J. M. and Robinson, P. T., 1979. Deep crustal drilling in the North Atlantic Ocean. *Science*, vol. 204, pp. 573–586.
14. Humphreys, D. R., 1988. Has the earth's magnetic field ever flipped? *Creation Research Society Quarterly*, vol. 25(3), pp. 130–137.
15. Inglis, D. R., 1981. Dynamo theory of the earth's varying magnetic field. *Reviews of Modern Physics*, vol. 53(3), pp. 481–496.
16. James, R. W., Roberts, P. H., and Winch, D. E., 1980. The Cowling anti-dynamo theorem. *Geophysical and Astrophysical Fluid Dynamics*, vol. 15, pp. 145–160.
17. Barnes, T. G., 1972. Young age vs. geologic age for the earth's magnetic field. *Creation Research*

Society Quarterly, vol. 9(1), pp. 47–50.

18. Humphreys, D. R., 1986. Reversals of the earth's magnetic field during the Genesis Flood. *Proceedings of the First International Conference on Creationism*, Creation Science Fellowship, Pittsburgh, vol. 2, pp. 113–126.

19. Barnes, T. G., Ref. 17.

20. Barnes, T. G., 1973. Electromagnetics of the earth's field and evaluation of electric conductivity, current, and joule heating. *Creation Research Society Quarterly*, vol. 9(4), pp. 222–230.

21. Humphreys, D. R., 1983. The creation of the earth's magnetic field. *Creation Research Society Quarterly*, vol. 20(1), pp. 89–94.

22. Humphreys, D. R., 1984. The creation of planetary magnetic fields. *Creation Research Society Quarterly*, vol. 21(2), pp. 140–149.

23. Humphreys, D. R., Ref. 18.

24. Wesson, P. S., 1972. Objections to continental drift and plate tectonics. *Journal of Geology*, vol. 80, pp. 185–197.

25. Noble, C. S. and Naughton, J. S., 1968. Deep-ocean basalts: inert gas content and uncertainties in age dating. *Science*, vol. 162, pp. 265–267.

26. Dalrymple, G. B. and Moore, J. G., 1968. Argon–40: excess in submarine pillow basalts from Kilauea Volcano, Hawaii. *Science*, vol. 161, pp. 1132–1135.

27. Scholl, D. W., Christensen, M. N., Von Huene, R., and Marlow, M. S., 1970. Peru-Chile trench sediments and sea-floor spreading. *Geological Society of America Bulletin*, vol. 81, pp. 1339–1360.

28. Von Huene, R., 1972. Structure of the continental margin and tectonism at the Eastern Aleutian Trench. *Geological Society of America Bulletin*, vol. 83, pp. 3613–3626.

29. Tanner, W. F., 1973. Deep-sea trenches and the compression assumption. *American Association of Petroleum Geologists Bulletin*, vol. 57, pp. 2195–2206.

30. Wesson, P. S., Ref. 24, p. 187.

31. Nevins, S. E., Ref. 2.

32. Carter, W. E. and Robertson, D. S., 1986. Studying the earth by very-long-baseline interferometry. *Scientific American*, vol. 255(5), pp. 44–52.

33. Carter, W. E. and Robertson, D. S., Ref. 32, pp. 44.

34. *Science News*, vol. 123(2), p. 20.

35. Carter, W. E. and Robertson, D. S., Ref. 32, p. 51.

36. Carter, W. E. and Robertson, D. S., Ref. 32, p. 52.

37. Carter, W. E. and Robertson, D. S., Ref. 32, p. 44.

38. Carter, W. E. and Robertson, D. S., Ref. 32, p. 52.

39. Carter, W. E. and Robertson, D. S., Ref. 32, p. 51.

40. Smith, D. E., 1989. Present-day motion of the earth's tectonic plates and associated deformation. *Geological Society of America, 1989 Annual Meeting, Abstracts with Programs*, pp. A120–121.

41. Wieland, C., 1983. An asteroid tilts the earth. *Ex Nihilo*, vol. 5(3), pp. 12–14.

42. Setterfield, B., 1983. An asteroid tilts the earth? Further evidence! *Ex Nihilo*, vol. 5(3), pp. 6–8.

43. Humphreys, D. R., Ref. 18.

44. Dewey, J. F., Pitman, W. C., Ryan, W. B. F. and Bonnin, J., 1973. Plate tectonics and the evolution of the Alpine System. *Geological Society of America Bulletin*, vol. 84, pp. 3137–3180.

45. Setterfield, B., 1987. Geological time and Scriptural chronology. Supplement to *The Atomic Constants, Light, and Time*, published by the author. We are informed that the work of the late South Australian Government Astronomer, George Dodwell, is being published by the University of Adelaide.

46. Maxwell, J. C., 1973. The new global tectonics. *Geotimes*, vol. 18(1), p. 31.

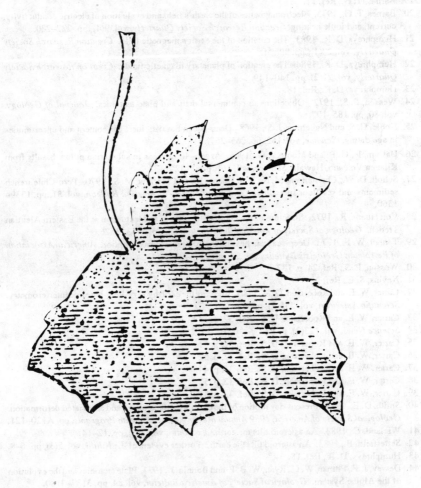

3

What about carbon-14 dating?

CARBON, that black substance in charred wood, comes in several forms. One less common form has atoms which are 14 times as heavy as hydrogen atoms. It is called carbon-14, or C^{14} for short. Unlike common carbon (C^{12}), carbon-14 disintegrates or 'falls to pieces' relatively easily. This instability makes it radioactive. Many people are concerned that C^{14} proves the biblical time-scale of history to be inaccurate. However, the C^{14} clock is in full accord with the biblical picture of earth's past.

Carbon-14, or radiocarbon as it is often called, is manufactured in the upper atmosphere by the action of cosmic rays. Ordinary nitrogen (N^{14}) is converted into C^{14} as shown in Figure 1.

Ordinary carbon (C^{12}) is found in the carbon dioxide in the air we breathe, which of course is cycled by plants and animals throughout nature, so that your body, or the leaf of a tree, or

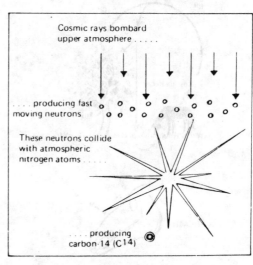

Cosmic rays bombard upper atmosphere . . . . .

. . . . producing fast moving neutrons

These neutrons collide with atmospheric nitrogen atoms . . . . .

. . . . producing carbon-14 (C^{14})

Fig. 1

even a piece of wooden furniture, contains carbon. When C^{14} has been formed, it behaves just like ordinary carbon (C^{12}), combining with oxygen to give carbon dioxide ($C^{14}O_2$), and also gets freely cycled through the cells of all plants and animals. The difference is this: once C^{14} has been formed, it begins to decay radioactively back to N^{14}, at a rate of change which can be measured. If we take a sample of air, and measure how many C^{12} atoms there are for every C^{14} atom, this is called the C^{14}/C^{12} ratio. Because C^{14} is so well 'mixed up' with the C^{12}, we expect to find that this ratio is the same if we sample a leaf from a tree, or a part of your body.

Think of it like a teaspoon of cocoa mixed into a cake dough — after a while, the 'ratio' of cocoa to flour particles would be roughly the same no matter which part of the cake you sampled. The fact that the C^{14} atoms are changing back to N^{14} doesn't matter in a living thing. Because it is constantly exchanging carbon with its surroundings, the 'mixture' will be the same as in the atmosphere and in all living things.

HOW THE 'CARBON CLOCK' WORKS

As soon as a plant or animal dies, however, the C^{14} atoms which decay are no longer replaced by new ones from outside, so the amount of C^{14} in that once living thing gets smaller and smaller as time goes on. Another way of saying it is that the C^{14}/C^{12} ratio gets smaller. In other words, we have a 'clock' which starts ticking at the moment something dies (Figure 2).

Obviously this works only for things which once contained carbon — it can't be used to date rocks and minerals, for example. We know how quickly C^{14} decays and so it becomes possible to measure how long it has been since the plant or animal died.

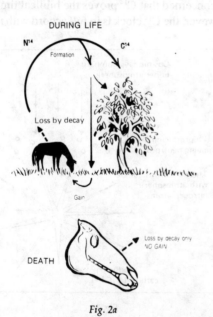

Fig. 2a

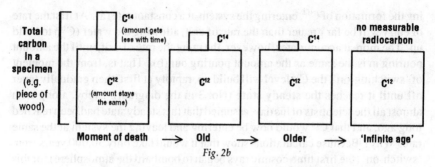

| Total carbon in a specimen (e.g. piece of wood) | C¹⁴ (amount gets less with time) C¹² (amount stays the same) | C¹⁴ C¹² | C¹⁴ C¹² | no measurable radiocarbon C¹² |

Moment of death → Old → Older → 'Infinite age'

Fig. 2b

THE KEY ASSUMPTION BEHIND THE METHOD

But wait — how do we know what the C^{14}/C^{12} ratio was to start with? We obviously need to know this to be able to work out at what point the 'clock' began to tick. We've seen that it would have been the same as in the atmosphere at the time the specimen died, so how do we know what that was? Do scientists assume that it was the same in the past as it is now? Well, not exactly. It is well known that the industrial revolution, with its burning of huge masses of coal, etc., has upset the natural carbon balance by releasing huge quantities of C^{12} into the air, for example. Tree-ring studies can tell us what the C^{14}/C^{12} ratio was like before the industrial revolution, and all radiocarbon dating is made with this in mind. How do we know what the ratio was before then, though, say thousands of years ago? It is assumed that the ratio has been constant for a very long time before the industrial revolution. Is this assumption correct (for on it hangs the whole validity of the system)? Why did W. F. Libby, the brilliant discoverer of this method, assume this? We know that C^{14} is continually entering the atmosphere (and hence the carbon cycle), and that C^{14} is continually leaving the system by its decay back to N^{14}. The more you have of a radioactive substance, the more there is to decay, that is, as more enters a system, the rate of leaving the system increases.

To understand this, let us use the example of a rainwater tank, representing the system, with evenly spaced holes in the sides (Figure 3). Let's switch on a tap at the top, represent-

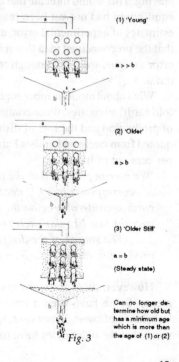

(1) 'Young'

$a >> b$

(2) 'Older'

$a > b$

(3) 'Older Still'

$a = b$

(Steady state)

Can no longer determine how old but has a minimum age which is more than the age of (1) or (2)

Fig. 3

ing the formation of C^{14}, entering the system at a constant rate (a). At first the rate of entry will be far greater than the rate of exit, allowing the water (C^{14}) to build up. The more it accumulates, however, the more the rate of exit, until the amount pouring in is the same as the amount pouring out (b). That is, from the moment of 'switching-on', the C^{14} level will build up, rapidly at first, then gradually taper off until it reaches the **steady state** (No. 3 in the diagram). Libby, along with almost all the scientists of his day, assumed that this steady state had been reached long ago, and that C^{14} would now be entering and leaving the system at the same rate. Why? Because calculations show that it would take only 30,000 years from 'switch-on' (the first time cosmic rays began to bombard the atmosphere) for this to happen, and of course geologists and others had by then long since persuaded most people that the earth was much, much older than that. In other words, C^{14} would have been in a steady state for many millions of years already, if the earth was that old.

WHAT DO MEASUREMENTS SHOW?

Was Libby right? In his day, measurements of which he was aware showed that C^{14} was entering the system some 12 per cent or more **faster** than it was leaving. This would indicate that the system was less than 30,000 years old, since equilibrium had not yet been reached. But the discrepancy was within Libby's estimates of experimental error, and so could be ignored. (Some have suggested that the preconceived idea that it had to be in equilibrium ensured that the given error margins were big enough to encompass the actual result, but this may be unfair.)

What about modern, more sophisticated measurements? Unfortunately for the 'old earth' advocates, these continue to support a real difference between the rate of production and the rate of disintegration. For instance, the following figures quoted from nuclear chemists Fairhall and Young suggest that it is as much as 50 per cent out of balance.

'We note in passing that the total natural C^{14} inventory of 2.16×10^{30} atoms . . . corresponds to a C^{14} decay rate of 1.63×10^4 disintegrations/$m^2 s$ of the earth, considerably below the estimated production rate of C^{14} atoms averaged over the last 10 solar cycles (111 years) of 2.5×10^4 ($\pm 0.5 \times 10^4$) atoms/$m^2 s$ . . . . The source of the discrepancy is . . . unknown unless the present day production rate is indeed significantly higher than the average production rate . . .'[1]

However, there are many complexities and inaccuracies in these measurements. Some have used a new, 'non-uniform' model based on an 'average' imbalance of some 35 per cent, to establish a 'recalibration scale' which would mean that the older dates have to be more greatly reduced than later ones. This seems in order at first glance, as does the use of the imbalance data to establish an upper limit to the age of the earth's atmosphere of some 7,000–10,000 years. However, one must proceed with great caution before stating this dogmatically, as the model may be too simplistic. For instance, how do we know that the 'mixing of cake dough' was really complete? Is the carbon in the top of the ocean in balance with that in the bottom? What are the possible errors in estimates of influx/outflow rates of C^{14}? And so on. Historic dates and tree-ring data suggest that the overall issues are more complex than may at first be thought.

OTHER FACTORS

We need to consider three other possible effects:

1. If, as most creationists propose, there was a vast water vapour canopy around the earth before the Flood, then this would have shielded the atmosphere from some of the cosmic radiation. Therefore, the amount of C^{14} in the pre-Flood

Part of a radiocarbon laboratory in which samples are prepared for testing.

world would have been significantly smaller than at present. So a specimen from before the Flood could appear to be 'very old' or even of 'infinite' age because it had so little C^{14} in it, making it look as if it had been decaying for tens of thousands of years. Most coal is vegetation that grew pre-Flood and was buried by the Flood, so it would therefore not be surprising to find that coal and oil, for example, would have virtually no radiocarbon activity to be measured.

2. The measured exponential decay of the earth's magnetic field as described by

Dr Thomas Barnes suggests that as you go back in history, the strength of the field increases rapidly. A stronger magnetic field would mean more protection against cosmic rays, therefore again much less C^{14} produced and again this gives artificially 'old' ages the more you go back in time.

3. Some recent, though controversial, research has raised the interesting suggestion that c (the speed of light) has decreased in historical times. During the 1930s and 1940s, the measurements seemed to be so consistently dropping that a controversy about declining c took place in the scientific literature for some time (see 'Doesn't distant starlight prove an old universe?', chapter 11, pp. 121–131). If it is correct, then radioactive decay rates would automatically be affected, and would show artificially high ages.

SUMMING UP

In summary then:

(a) The C^{14} on earth is not in a steady state, but is building up. This is not in accord with predictions based upon belief in a very old atmosphere.

(b) On the basis of the presently available evidence, the oldest radiocarbon dates have to be adjusted from the apparently incorrect 'uniform' model which is still in use today, and when this is done there is a shrinking in these dates. The older the date, the greater the reduction.

(c) The protective water vapour canopy and the greater magnetic field before the Flood could mean that C^{14} levels in the past were significantly smaller than at present, thus causing erroneous results.

(d) Any systematic change in atomic constants (e.g. a faster 'c' at any time in the past) would also effectively reduce radioactive ages.

EMBARRASSMENT FROM YOUNG DATES

In any case, even the incorrect 'uniform' model has given, in many cases, serious embarrassment to the evolutionist by giving ages which are much younger than those he expects in terms of his model of earth history. Consider this — if a specimen is older than 50,000 years, it has been calculated that it would have such a small amount of C^{14} that for practical purposes it would show an 'infinite' radiocarbon age. So it was expected that most deposits such as coal, gas, etc. would be undatable by this method. In fact, of thousands of dates in the journals *Radiocarbon* and *Science* to 1968, only a handful were classed 'undatable' —most were of the sort which should have been in this category. This is especially remarkable with samples of coal and gas supposedly produced in the Carboniferous period 300 million years ago! Some examples of dates which contradict orthodox (evolutionary) views:

- Coal from Russia from the 'Pennsylvanian', supposedly 300 million years old, was dated at 1,680 years.[2]
- Natural gas from Alabama and Mississippi (Cretaceous and Eocene respectively) — should have been 50 million to 135 million years old, yet C^{14} gave dates of 30,000 to 34,000 years respectively.[3]
- Bones of a sabre-toothed tiger from the LaBrea tar pits (near Los Angeles), supposedly 100,000–one million years old, gave a date of 28,000 years.[4]

OTHER C^{14} 'CLANGERS'

In addition to the above effects, which are more or less systematic, there are other possible sources of error in C^{14} dating. In the light of all this, it would be foolhardy indeed to insist that a C^{14} date represents absolute truth, especially if it contradicts the clear teaching of Scripture. Consider these examples of C^{14} results:

- A freshly killed seal dated by C^{14} showed it had 'died' 1300 years ago.[5]
- Living mollusc shells were 'dated' at up to 2,300 years old.[6]
- Living snails' shells showed they had 'died' 27,000 years ago.[7]

We hasten to add that one can usually retrospectively find out the reasons for these sorts of anomalous results — for example, the C^{14} activity in dissolved carbonates in the water, etc. But when testing a sample of unknown age from a largely unknown environment at the time of its death, how can we exclude similar sorts of effects?

A quotation from a respected anthropological journal highlights the nature of the problem:

'The troubles of the radiocarbon dating method are undeniably deep and serious . . . It should be no surprise, then, that fully half of the dates are rejected. The wonder is, surely, that the remaining half come to be accepted.'[8]

In overview, we see that the radiocarbon dating method is certainly no embarrassment to

Could living snails have died 27,000 years ago?

the biblical creationist who believes in a young earth. In fact, when fully understood in accord with modern data, it seems to give support to this position.

FOOTNOTES

1. Fairhall, A. W. and Young, J. A., 1970. Radionuclides in the Environment. *Advances in Chemistry*, vol. 93, p. 402.
2. *Radiocarbon*, vol. 8 (1966).
3. *Radiocarbon*, vol. 8 (1966). Many of the earlier radiocarbon dates on objects such as coal and gas, which should be 'undatable', have been attributed to contamination from, for example, worker's fingerprints, etc. Dr Gerald Aardsma, physicist at the Institute for Creation Research, is currently working on the construction of an apparatus, using existing technology, to look for very low levels of C^{14} activity in, for example, coal after excluding contamination. Such low-level activity would not be expected on the basis of 'old earth' theory and so is not looked for at present.
4. *Radiocarbon*, vol. 10 (1968).
5. *Antarctic Journal*, vol. 6 (September–October 1971), p. 211.
6. *Science*, vol. 141 (1963), pp. 634–637.
7. *Science*, vol. 224 (1984), pp. 58–61.
8. Lee, R. E., 1981. Radiocarbon, Ages in Error. *Anthropological Journal of Canada*, vol. 19, No. 3, p. 9.

4

Were there really ice ages?

THE only unequivocal evidence we have for ice ages is for one, which usually correlates with the most recent one on the evolutionist's time-scale, in the so-called Pleistocene epoch. This was immediately prior to the Recent epoch in which man has left written records.

This Ice Age is believed by evolutionists to have started about two million years ago and terminated about 11,000 years ago. Most creationists, on the other hand, believe the Ice Age began soon after the Flood and continued for less than a millennium.

EARLIER ICE AGES?

Evolutionists have proposed that there were earlier ice ages, for example in the late Precambrian and the Permian of the so-called geological column. However, the evidence is ambiguous because tenuous comparisons of sedimentary rocks in those geological systems with varved sediments and tillites of the Ice Age are open to other interpretations/explanations.

Varves, for instance, are thin, rhythmic silt and clay layers that are usually thought to represent slow sedimentary processes of deposition within a glacial lake below a glacier. Each couplet of layers is considered to represent annual repetitions under summer and winter transport of sediments into the lake. However, Lambert and Hsu have presented evidence from a Swiss Lake that these varve-layers form rapidly by catastrophic, turbid water underflows.[1] At one location five couplets of these 'varves' formed during a single year. At Mount St Helens in the USA, a 25 feet (7.6 metre) thick stratified deposit consisting of many thin laminae akin to varves was formed in less than one day (June 12, 1980).[2] Furthermore, other evidence such as striated (scratched) rock pavements, for example, in the Adelaide area of Australia, are not the conclusive evidence for earlier Ice Ages that they are so often claimed to be.[3]

The effects of **the** Ice Age are still with us, particularly the polar ice caps, the alpine glaciers, and the numerous glacial landforms and sediments. Because these effects are seen on the current land surface, it is quite clear that the Ice Age occurred soon after the Flood.

During the Ice Age, a great continental ice sheet, centred somewhere in the north-east Canada–Greenland area, swept down over North America, reaching as far south as the northern United States and carving out the Great Lakes in the process. Other effects left behind by the ice include great mounds (or moraines), of unsorted sand, gravel and boulders (tillite), scratches and grooves (striations) on bedrock pavements and 'varved' glacial sediments in outwashed lakes. A similar ice sheet swept over northern Europe from Scandinavia south to Germany, France, Italy and England. In the North American Rockies, the European Alps and other mountain chains, permanent ice caps rested on the summits and extensive valley glaciers descended down almost to the plains below.

Yet another ice sheet covered parts of the southern hemisphere, spreading

The effects of the Ice Age are still with us, particularly the polar ice caps, the alpine glaciers, and the numerous glacial landforms and sediments.

from Antarctica to cover New Zealand, Tasmania, parts of south-eastern mainland Australia and southern Chile. Some glaciers still remain in the southern Alps of New Zealand's South Island, but glacial landforms are all that are left high in New South Wales's Snowy Mountains and in Tasmania's rugged interior, west and south-west, as a reminder of the action of the ice sheet during the Ice Age.

In just about all textbooks we read that geologists believe that the Ice Age involved at least three advances and retreats of the ice, with warm periods (called inter-glacials) in between. However, the evidence for the earlier advances, for example, in North America, is of an entirely different sort from the moraines and

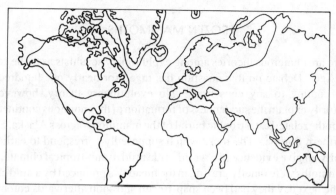

During the Ice Age a great continental sheet of ice, centred somewhere in the north–east Canada–Greenland region, swept down into North America. Similar ice sheets swept over northern Europe and parts of the southern hemisphere.

striations of the last one. The dense clay soils, old river terraces and other phenomena, interpreted as evidence for the earlier advances, can be interpreted as water-laid formations more easily than they can as being the result of earlier glaciations.

HUMAN OCCUPATION

It is important to note that the ice never covered the entire earth, contrary to the mental picture that some people have. The ice never covered more than a third of the earth's surface even at its greatest suggested extent. At the same time as there was the 'glacial period' in the upper latitudes, there was probably a period of higher rainfall in the lower latitudes. Such higher rainfall in the lower latitudes would have assured an abundant water supply even in such present-day desert areas as the Sahara, the Gobi, and Arabia. Indeed, archaeological excavations have yielded abundant evidences of human occupation and complex irrigation economies in these now desolate regions.

There is much evidence of human occupation in these lower latitudes throughout the entire Ice Age. The Neanderthal peoples, for instance, seem to have lived near the edge of the ice sheet in Europe, and many anthropologists now believe that their somewhat brutish appearance was due to disease (rickets, arthritis) contracted because of the cold, damp and poorly sunlit climates characteristic of such regions at that time.

There is no reason (apart from highly questionable dating methods) why these peripheral cultures could not have been contemporaneous with the advanced civilizations of Egypt, Babylonia, and others that were developing in the lower latitudes. The Ice Age can easily be understood as lasting several hundred years rather than two million years.

FROZEN MAMMOTHS

There are numerous theories among evolutionary scientists as to the cause of the Ice Age. Debate on this question has raged for nearly one hundred years without coming to any consensus. No evolutionary theory, however, can satisfactorily explain the suddenness of formation of the enormous continental ice sheets, or the related catastrophic burial of the mammoths across Alaska, Siberia, and Northern Europe. The rocks which supposedly correspond to earlier ages practically all give evidence of a world-wide mild or sub-tropical climate, so one day mammoths were quietly grazing in the meadows produced by a mild climate, but by the next day they had been snap-frozen and soon afterwards entombed in ice and mud.

The mystery of these frozen giants, the mammoths, is illustrative of the insurmountable problems facing any evolutionary and uniformitarian theory as to the cause of the Ice Age. Many of these great hairy extinct elephants are found apparently snap-frozen in the permafrost (frozen muck). There were some, for instance the famous Beresovka mammoth, that had food remaining in their mouths and stomachs. The skin of the mammoths shows that they were almost certainly not particularly adapted to Arctic conditions any more than the great cats, bison, wolves, bears and horses which have been found buried in the same layers. Thus, when we think of mammoths, there is no reason to see them as necessarily associated with ice while they were alive. Mammoth bones have been found in Mexico.

Some of the plant species identified in the stomach of the Beresovka mammoth are not now growing so far north. To prevent the stomach juices digesting these plant remains, the freezing of at least the Beresovka mammoth had to be extremely severe and rapid.

The bones of millions of mammoths (and other creatures found with them) are buried in Europe, Alaska and Siberia. Where the ground is no longer frozen, there is no associated flesh. Where it is now permanently frozen (with not enough vegetation growing these days to support great herds of animals anyway) excavation of the bones is usually associated with rotting flesh to varying degrees. Although most of the mammoth flesh is found in small scraps, about forty fairly intact frozen carcasses have been studied by scientists so far.[4]

From this kind of evidence one thing is clear. The snap-freezing of these mammoths cannot be accounted for within the many uniformitarian and evolutionary geology explanations for the onset of the Ice Age over tens or hundreds of years.

BIBLICAL EXPLANATION

But what evolutionary geology, with its 'slow and gradual' bias, can't accommodate and finds inexplicable, the biblical record of catastrophic change at the time of the Flood explains quite satisfactorily. The Scriptures imply that before the Flood, the world had pleasant topography and climate everywhere, the latter probably involving the 'greenhouse effect' produced by a vast thermal blanket of invisible water vapour (the 'waters above the firmament' mentioned in Genesis 1:7). There were no rainstorms, no volcanic eruptions, no earthquakes, no blizzards or physical disturbances of any kind — the world had been prepared to be 'very good' (Genesis 1:31) as a home for man and the animals.

With the Flood, however, all this changed. The vapour canopy condensed and fell to the ground in violent torrents for 40 days, and waters and magmas burst forth all over the earth through 'the fountains of the great deep' (probably volcanoes) for five long months (150 days) (Genesis 7:11; 8:2). Tremendous earth movements accompanied and followed the Flood, and catastrophic phenomena of all kinds continued on a lesser scale after the Flood.

Did this freezing, therefore, which produced the polar ice caps and the snap-freezing of the mammoths, occur shortly after the world-wide Flood had buried millions of these animals into the now permanently frozen muck? Or did it occur as a result of some massive post-Flood catastrophe, perhaps in the 'days of Peleg' when 'the earth was divided' (Genesis 10:25)? Suggestions for the mechanism of freezing have included an asteroid impact hypothesis, the collapse of the pre-Flood vapour canopy, and also a sudden 'dumping' of ice from a massive cometary visitor.

Whatever the exact answer, it is clear that there was a **rapid and permanent** change in the climate of a vast region of the earth, associated with the death of countless millions of animals in a massive frozen graveyard in which the soil never thaws.

Of the possible mechanisms that triggered the Ice Age, the precipitation of the water vapour blanket at the outset of the Flood most certainly did occur, and in so doing gradually dissipated the greenhouse effect so that the Arctic and Antarctic zones grew bitterly cold. During and immediately after the Flood the tremendous heat energy released from the depths would have evaporated great quantities of water, much of which was transported to the polar regions by the newly developing post-Flood atmospheric circulation, where it fell as great quantities of snow. Soon the accumulating snow pack would have become an ice sheet, which would have radiated out from its centre.

Large amounts of volcanic dust from residual volcanic eruptions following the Flood would most likely have remained in the atmosphere, generating a large temperature drop over land by reflecting much solar radiation back into space. Furthermore, such volcanic dust would most likely have been replenished in the atmosphere for hundreds of years following the Flood, due to continued widespread post-Flood volcanism, as evidenced by the vast quantities of volcanic rocks among the sediments of the immediate post-Flood era (possibly the so-called Tertiary and Pleistocene). Such additional processes would have added to the atmospheric, land and sea surface temperature losses that would have thus speeded up the formation of the continental ice sheets.

Interestingly, there seem to be certain references to this Ice Age in the ancient book of Job (37:9–10; 38:22–23, 29–30), who perhaps lived in its waning years. (Job lived in the land of Uz, Uz being a descendant of Shem [Genesis 10], so that most conservative biblical scholars agree that Job probably lived at some time between the Tower of Babel and Abraham.) The Lord questioned Job from a whirlwind, 'Out of whose womb came the ice? And the hoary frost of heaven, who hath gendered it? The waters are hid as with a stone, and the face of the deep is frozen' (Job 38:29–30). Such questions presuppose Job knew, either by firsthand experience or by historical/family records, what the Lord was talking about. There is little doubt that this is a reference to both the suddenness of the Ice Age and its effects.

THE AFTERMATH

The land surfaces that had arisen from underneath the Flood waters were of course devoid of any plants, the pre-Flood land surfaces having been denuded of their plants, eroded and/or buried. The carbon dioxide content of the atmosphere had also probably been reduced by the upheavals of the Flood (the Flood waters dissolving a lot of carbon dioxide, plus still more being incorporated in precipitating calcium carbonate as limestones). Gradually, however, the seeds and twigs

that had survived from the antediluvian plants became rooted and grew again, while the multiplying biota began again to emit carbon dioxide into the atmosphere. Great peat bogs certainly developed along the ice sheet margins, and peat bog vegetation is known to be especially effective in supplying large amounts of carbon dioxide to the atmosphere. By these processes, eventually enough of this gas built up in the atmosphere to cause the temperatures to rise sufficiently to begin melting the ice and causing it to retract to its present-day position.

During the centuries of the Ice Age, many of the great animals that had come off the Ark, though they survived and proliferated for a time, eventually were unable to cope with the drastic changes in climate and environment and became extinct, some, such as the mammoths, as a result of the catastrophism associated with these drastic changes. As the ice later retreated and the rainfall patterns changed yet again, many of the pluviated (well-watered) regions became arid and so even more animals died out. The great cataclysm of the Flood, followed by the smaller related catastrophes of glaciation, vulcanism, and eventual desiccation (drying out), drastically changed the character of the earth and its inhabitants.

FOOTNOTES

1. Lambert, A. and Hsu, K. J., 1979. Non-annual cycles of varve-like sedimentation in Walensee, Switzerland. *Sedimentology*, vol. 26, pp. 453–461.
2. Austin, S.A., 1986. Mount St Helens and catastrophism. *Proceedings of the First International Conference on Creationism*, Creation Science Fellowship, Pittsburgh, vol. 1, pp. 3–9.
3. This is **not** to say that these striations on rock pavements were not carved by ice, since the glaciation of the Ice Age could have been responsible, thus making it unnecessary to postulate any earlier Ice Ages.
4. The most interesting and comprehensive compilation of the available information relating to the frozen mammoths is found in a major section of the book *The Waters Above*, by Dr Joseph C. Dillow, Moody Press, Chicago (1981).

NOTE: During compilation of this article use was made of Dr Henry Morris's article 'The Ice Age', *Creation Ex Nihilo*, vol. 11(2), 1989, pp. 10–12. Due acknowledgment is given.

5

Why did God take six days?

WHEN one takes up a Bible, reads Genesis chapter 1, and takes it at face value, it seems to say that God created the world, the universe and everything in them in six ordinary (approximately 24-hour) days. However, there is a view in our churches that has become prevalent over the years that these 'days' could have been thousands, millions or even billions of years in duration. Does it really matter what length these days were anyway? Is it possible to determine whether or not they were ordinary days or in fact long periods of time?

WHY 'LONG DAYS'?

The main reason why many try to make the Genesis days into long periods is to find a way to harmonize the creation account with the idea that there was a succession of vast geological 'ages' before man appeared. But if one accepts these 'ages' as being real, then one is accepting that interpretation of the fossil record which (1) denies a world-wide Flood (since such a Flood would have wiped out all traces of such preceding 'ages') and (2) insists that there were many creatures which lived, struggled and died out long before man appeared on the scene. This, of course, seriously undermines the whole New Testament/Gospel emphasis relating to sin, death, bloodshed, Redemption and the Curse.[1]

Put simply, any attempt to harmonize long geological ages with Genesis (gap theory, day-age theory, progressive creation, etc.) inevitably means accepting death before man, rather than the New Testament insistence that the struggle, suffering and bloodshed of the present world came about AFTER Adam sinned. That these attempts to compromise are artificial, and not true to the text, can be seen by the following quotation from Dr James Barr (Regius Professor of Hebrew, at Oxford University).

> *'So far as I know, there is no professor of Hebrew or Old Testament at any world-class university who does not believe that the writer(s) of Gen. 1–11 intended to convey to their readers the ideas that (a) creation took place in a series of six days which were the same as the days of 24 hours we now experience (b) the figures contained in the Genesis genealogies provided by simple addition a chronology from the beginning of the world up to later stages in the biblical story (c) Noah's flood was understood to be world-wide and extinguish all human and animal life except for those in the ark.'*[2]

Note that the experts are not saying they BELIEVE the account; they are just dealing honestly with what it actually says, with the realities of the language.

WHAT IS A 'DAY'?

The word for 'day' in Genesis 1 is the Hebrew word *yom*. It can mean either a day (in the ordinary 24-hour sense), the daylight portion (say about 12 hours) of an ordinary 24-hour day (i.e. 'day' as distinct from 'night'), or occasionally an indefinite period of time (e.g. 'In the time of the Judges' or 'In the day of the Lord'). Without exception, in the Hebrew Old Testament the word *yom* is never used to refer to a definite long period of time with specific beginning and end points. Furthermore, it is important to note that even when the word *yom* is used in the indefinite sense, it is clearly indicated by the context that the literal meaning of the word 'day' is not intended.

Some people say that the word 'day' in Genesis may have been used symbolically and so we are not meant to take it literally. However, an important point that many fail to consider is that a word can never be used symbolically the first time it is used! In fact, a word can be used symbolically only when it first has a literal meaning. In the New Testament we are told that Jesus is the 'door'. We know what this means because we know that the word 'door' means an entrance. Because we understand its literal meaning it is able to be applied in a symbolic sense to Jesus Christ. The word 'door' could not be used in this way unless it first had the literal meaning we understand it to have. Thus, the word 'day' cannot be used symbolically the first time it is used in the book of Genesis. Indeed, this is why the author of Genesis has gone to great lengths to carefully define the word 'day' the first time it appears. In Genesis 1:4 we read that God separated the 'light from the darkness'. Then in Genesis 1:5 we read, *'God called the light Day, and the darkness he called Night.'* In other words, the terms were being very carefully defined. The first time the word 'day' is used it is defined as 'the light' to distinguish it from 'the darkness' called 'night'. Genesis 1:5 then finishes off with, 'And the evening and the morning were the first day.' This is the same phrase used for each of the other five days and shows that there was a clearly established cycle of days and nights (i.e. periods of light and periods of darkness). The periods of light on each of the six days were when God did His work, and the periods of darkness were when God did no creative work.

A DAY AND THE SUN

But how could there be day and night if the sun wasn't in existence? After all, it is clear from Genesis 1 that the sun was not created until the fourth day. Now Genesis 1:3 tells us that God created light on the first day, and the phrase 'evening and morning' shows there were alternating periods of light and darkness. Therefore, light was in existence, being directed from one stationary source upon a rotating earth, resulting in the day and night cycle. However, we are not told exactly where this light came from. The word for 'light' in Genesis 1:3 means that the substance of light was created. Then in Genesis 1:14–19 we are told of the creation on the fourth day of the sun which was to be the source of light from that time onwards.

The sun was created to rule the day that already existed. The day stayed the same. It merely had a new light source. The first three days of creation (before

Ptolemy of Alexandria (AD 85–165) believed that the sun, moon, planets and stars revolved around a stationary earth in a series of inter-layered spheres.

the sun) were the same type of days as the three days with the sun.

One of the possible reasons God deliberately left the creation of the sun until the fourth day is because He knew that, down through the ages, cultures would try to worship the sun as the source of life. Not only this, modern-day theories tell us that the sun came before the earth. God is showing us He made the earth and light to start with, that He can sustain it with its day and night cycle, and that the sun was created on the fourth day as a tool of His to be the bearer of light from that time.

Probably one of the major reasons people have tended not to take the days of Genesis as ordinary days, is because they have believed scientists have proved the earth to be billions of years old. But this is not true. There is no absolute age-dating method to determine exactly how old the earth is. Besides, there is a lot of evidence consistent with a belief in a young age for the earth, perhaps only thousands of years.[3]

WHY SIX DAYS?

God is an infinite being. This means He has infinite power, infinite knowledge, infinite wisdom, etc. Obviously, God could make anything He wanted to in no time at all — He could have created the whole universe, the earth and all it contains in no time at all. Perhaps the question we should be asking is why did God take as long as six days anyway? After all, six days is a long time for an infinite being to take to make anything! The answer can be found in Exodus 20:11.

Exodus 20 contains the Ten Commandments. It should be remembered that these commandments were written on stone by the very 'finger of God', for in Exodus we read, '*And when he had made an end of speaking with him on Mount Sinai, he gave Moses two tablets of the Testimony, tablets of stone, written with the finger of God*' (Exodus 31:18). The fourth commandment in verse 9 of chapter 20 tells us that we are to work six days and rest for one. The justification for this is given in verse 11, '*For in six days the Lord made the heavens and the earth, the sea and all that is in them and rested the seventh day. Therefore the Lord blessed the Sabbath day and hallowed it*'. This is a direct reference to God's creation week in Genesis 1. To be consistent (and we must be), whatever is used as the meaning of the word 'day' in Genesis 1 must also be used here. If you are going to say the word 'day' means a long period of time in Genesis, then it has been already shown that the only way this can be is in the sense that the 'day' is an indefinite or indeterminate period of time — **not** a definite period of time. Thus the sense of Exodus 20:9–11 would have to be 'six indefinite periods shalt thou labour, and rest a seventh indefinite period'! This however makes no sense at all. By accepting the days as ordinary days we understand that God is telling us that He

worked for six ordinary days and rested for one ordinary day to set a pattern for man — the pattern of our seven-day week which we still have today! In other words, here in Exodus 20 we learn the reason why God took as long as six days to make everything — He was setting a pattern for us to follow, a pattern we still follow today.

DAY-AGE INCONSISTENCIES

There are many inconsistencies for those who accept the days in Genesis as long periods of time. For instance, we are told in Genesis 1:26–28 that God made the first man (Adam) on the sixth day. Adam lived through the rest of the sixth day, through the seventh day, and then we are told in Genesis 5:5 that he died when he was 930 years old. (We are not still in the seventh day now as some people misconstrue the account, for Genesis 2:2 tells us God '**rested**' from His work of creation, not that He is **resting** from His work of creation.) If each day was, for example, a million years, then there are real problems. In fact, if each day was only a thousand years long this still makes no sense of Adam's age at death either!

A DAY IS AS A THOUSAND YEARS

But some refer to 2 Peter 3:8 which tells us,
'With the Lord one day is as a thousand years, and a thousand years as one day.'
This verse is used by many who teach, by inference at least, that the days in Genesis must each be a thousand years long. This reasoning, however, is quite wrong. Turning to Psalm 90:4, we read a very similar verse,
'For a thousand years in your sight are like yesterday when it is passed, and like a watch in the night.'
In both 2 Peter 3 and Psalm 90 the whole context is that God is limited neither by natural processes nor by time. God is 'outside' time, for He also 'created' time. Neither verse refers to the days of creation in Genesis, for they are dealing with God's not being bound by time. In 2 Peter 3, the context is in relation to Christ's second coming, pointing out the fact that with God a day is just like a thousand years or a thousand years is just like one day — that God is unaffected by time. This has nothing to do with the days of creation in Genesis!

Furthermore, in 2 Peter 3:8 the word 'day' is being contrasted with 'a thousand years'. The word 'day' thus has a literal meaning which enables it to be contrasted with 'a thousand years'. It could not be contrasted with 'a thousand years' if it didn't have a literal meaning. That is, the word 'day' is not being defined here but is being contrasted with the phrase 'a thousand years'. Thus the thrust of the Apostle's message is that God can do in a very short time what men or 'nature' would require a very long time (if ever) to accomplish. Evolutionists try to make out that the chance, random processes of 'nature' required millions of years to produce man. Many Christians have accepted these millions of years, added them to the Bible, and then said that God took millions of years to make everything. However, the point of 2 Peter 3:8 is that God is not limited by time whereas evolution requires time (and lots of it).

It is also important to note that in the section of 2 Peter preceding the statement that *'one day is as a thousand years'*, we are told that

'. . . *scoffers will come in the last days, walking according to their own lusts, and saying, "Where is the promise of his coming? For since the fathers fell asleep, **all things continue as they were from the beginning of creation."***' (2 Peter 3:3–4).

Thus, in the last days people are going to say that things have just gone on and on — just as the evolutionists say things have gone on and on for millions of years. These people do not believe that God intervenes in history. This statement '. . . all things continue as they were from the beginning of creation' could really be defined as the modern-day concept of 'uniformitarianism'. This is the view prevalent in geology today that 'the present is the key to the past' (i.e. this world has gone on and on for millions of years in the same way as we see things happening today). This is really the basis of modern evolutionary geology. Most modern-day geologists don't believe that God created the world thousands of years ago but that it is a product of processes over millions of years. God told us quite clearly that He created everything in six days and that He took this long to do it because of the particular purposes explained in Exodus 20.

DAY AND YEARS

In Genesis 1:14 we read that God said,

'Let there be lights in the firmament of the heavens to divide the day from the night; and let them be for signs and seasons, and for days and years'.

If the word 'day' here is not a literal day, then the word 'years' being used in the same verse would be meaningless!

DAY AND COVENANT

Turning to Jeremiah 33:25–26 we read,

'Thus says the Lord: "If my covenant is not with day and night and if I have not appointed the ordinances of heaven and earth, then will I cast away the descendants of Jacob and David my servant so that I will not take any of his descendants to be rulers over the descendants of Abraham, Isaac and Jacob. For I will cause their captives to return and will have mercy on them."'

The Lord here is telling Jeremiah that He has a covenant with the day and the night which cannot be broken because it is related to the promise to the descendants of David — including the one who was promised to take the throne (Christ). Now this covenant between God and day and night began in Genesis 1, for God first defined day and night when He spoke them into existence. So if this covenant between the day and the night does not exist when God clearly says it does (i.e. if you don't take Genesis 1 to literally mean six ordinary days), then this promise given here through Jeremiah is invalid.

DOES THE DAY MATTER?

Finally, does it really matter whether we accept them as ordinary days or not? The answer is a most definite 'Yes'! It is really a principle of how one approaches the Bible. For instance, if we

don't accept them as ordinary days, then we have to ask the question, 'What are they?' The answer is, 'We don't know.' If we approach the days in this way, logically it follows that we should then approach other passages of Genesis in the same way (i.e. be consistent). For instance, when it says God took dust and made Adam — what does this mean? If it does not mean what it says then we don't know what it means! It is therefore important to take Genesis literally. Furthermore, it should be noted that you cannot 'interpret literally', for a 'literal interpretation' is a contradiction in terms. You either take it literally or you interpret it! It is important to realize we should take it literally unless it is obviously symbolic, and when it is so the context will make it quite clear or we will be told so in the text.

If a person accepts that we don't know what the word 'day' means in Genesis, then can another person who says they are literal days be accused of being wrong? The answer is 'no' because the person who accepts them as ordinary days does know what they mean. Rather, it is the other person, who doesn't know what the days mean, who cannot accuse anyone of being wrong!

When people accept at face value what Genesis is teaching, and accept the days as ordinary days, they will have no problems in understanding what the rest of Genesis is all about.

'For in six days the Lord made the heavens and the earth, the sea, and all that is in them, but He rested on the seventh day. Therefore the Lord blessed the Sabbath day and hallowed it' (Exodus 20:11).

FOOTNOTES

1. See Ken Ham's *The Lie: Evolution*, Master Books, San Diego (1987).
2. Prof. James Barr in a personal letter dated 23 April 1984 to David C. C. Watson.
3. For a summary of the problems with dating methods and evidence for a young earth, see the publication *Bone of Contention* by Sylvia Baker, published by Creation Science Foundation Ltd, P.O. Box 302, Sunnybank, Qld 4109, Australia, or obtainable in the USA from Institute for Creation Research, P.O. Box 2667, El Cajon, CA 92021. For a layman's summary of even more evidences, see *It's a Young World After All* by Paul Ackerman, obtainable from Creation Science Foundation Ltd.

6

How did 'bad things' come about?

'THE world before the Fall had no death or struggle. Nowadays, many creatures have equipment which is apparently designed to attack, hurt, trap, kill or eat others, or to defend themselves against such things. For example, the poison-injecting fangs of snakes, the great meat-eating cats and the spider's web, to name just a few. So when and how did these things, which are suited to a fallen world but were unnecessary before the Fall, come to be?'

There is no single position which would be agreed upon by all creationists in answer to this, so we will briefly look at the merits of a number of possibilities.

First, we need to look at those clear teachings of Scripture which bear on this question, remembering that the Bible gives us true, but not exhaustive, information. We may then try to fill in the gaps in our knowledge by reasoning, which will probably always have to be largely speculative, using the known facts about the living world. The Scriptures teach:

(a) There was no death and struggle in the animal kingdom before the Fall. God did not ascribe the life-principle (Hebrew *nephesh*, often translated 'soul') to plants. So Adam's eating a carrot did not involve death in the biblical sense. Perhaps the *nephesh* refers to self-conscious life. This raises the question of very simple creatures which are still technically animals — for example, the bacteria which today die in countless numbers every second, or the one-celled amoebae. By today's biological definition, at such a level, the difference between a 'plant' and an 'animal' may be little more than the presence or absence of chloroplasts (tiny bodies in the cell fluid containing the necessary chemicals to extract useful energy from sunlight). Does this mean that those without chloroplasts have 'life' in the biblical sense, but those with them do not? Many have suggested that the *nephesh* may not be present in such simpler organisms, but the Bible is not specific about this. If it is so, then bacteria may have been dying (as well as reproducing) in Eden before the Fall. We would have no way of knowing from Scripture exactly where the cut-off point was — for instance, do ants qualify as being capable of 'death' in this sense? Scripture makes the statement 'the life of the flesh is in the blood' (Leviticus 17:11. See also Genesis 9:4). If we use this to classify organisms into those with or without such '*nephesh*-life', it is helpful up to a point, but there are still difficulties as to what counts as blood in some of the simpler insects and crustaceans. The presence of haemoglobin cannot be definitive, as it is found even in some plants.

It can be safely said, however, that there was none of what we might call violent death, especially that involving bloodshed. In other words, those we would generally mean, in everyday usage, by the word 'animals' were not fighting, killing, shedding the blood of others and eating them, as many do today.

(b) The world will one day be restored (Acts 3:21) to a state in which, once again,

there will be no such death and violence in the animal kingdom. Whether Isaiah 11:6–9 is taken to be referring to the millennial kingdom or the new heavens and earth, the point is the same. Lambs, wolves, leopards, kids, bears and calves will all dwell together peacefully. Lions will once again be plant-eaters.

(c) There was no meat-eating before the Fall (Genesis 1:29–30), whether by man or animal.

(d) Man was permitted to eat meat only after the Flood (Genesis 9:3). This may have been due to the extinction of many plant species which were formerly able to easily provide all the protein requirements for humans. To be well

nourished by a totally vegetable diet today is difficult, though not impossible. Of course, men may have eaten animals anyway even before God gave permission. If that did happen, then it was probably not widespread, because Scripture implies that the animals had minimal fear of man before the Flood (Genesis 9:2).

To return, then, to our question with the above in mind. Animals today have certain pieces of biological equipment which they use either to attack others, or to defend themselves. Let's group these together and call them 'defence-attack structures' (DAS). The first question is: Were they created as such, designed to do harm, for instance?

The next, related question is: When did they come about? They would seem to have been quite out of place in a pre-Fall world.

The following are some of the possible answers which have been given, along with a discussion of some of the difficulties.

POSITION No. 1

'Those things that are now used as DAS were not designed for this purpose, and had a different function pre-Fall. They reached their present function by degeneration — for example, mutations.'

One can point to the fact that some creatures alive today have sharp teeth that look as if they would be used to rip meat, but we know they don't use them for that. The fruit bat is a prime example. So, the argument goes, could not the lion's teeth have been used to chew fruit before the Fall? Viruses which today inject harmful genetic material into their hosts may have had a useful pre-Fall role.[1]

Perhaps other 'harmful' structures had a different function pre-Fall, which has been lost or modified, either by choice[2] or (the explanation usually given) by degenerate mutations.

The living giant panda has sharp teeth and claws, and yet uses them to rip off and eat plant (bamboo) material. Occasionally they have been observed to eat small animals. If, by the time man first observed them, most pandas ate animals, we would find it hard to imagine that their teeth and claws originally were for the purpose of eating plants.

Position No. 1 avoids the problem of a good God's designing 'harmful' structures.[3] However, difficulties arise if this position is used to explain all occurrences of DAS. Virtually all creatures have some form of DAS, even if only a highly sensitive nervous system for warning of attack. They certainly give every indication of being 'designed to cope' in a fallen world. Most of these DAS show great evidence of complex and specific design.

In fact, most, if not all, of the examples used by creationists to show design in living things involve DAS. If we say that DAS, or at least some aspects of their present function, arose by chance mutations, then we may have seriously undermined the main argument from design. It would mean that we would be saying that millions of different, complex and intricate patterns came about by chance. Think of the engineering marvel of a spider's web, some of which are used by them to trap birds. All the complex machinery to make these webs is coupled with programmed instincts (which programming involves coded information) to tell the spiders where to build them for best hunting results, and when and how to move in for the kill on to the trapped prey. In literally millions of examples, since we would maintain that complex, purposive design means intelligent, purposive creation, there is *prima facie* evidence of God's having purposely designed the DAS as well.

The other problem is that this would mean that in each case of an **observed** DAS, the 'true' (pre-Fall) function was something different. It may be argued that our ignorance of the pre-Fall function does not mean that there wasn't one. This is true, of course, but if used for each and every one of the millions of DAS, risks stretching credulity to the limit. One should also not overlook the full extent of what is involved in any particular defence-attack mechanism. For instance, discussions on the shape of teeth and claws may overlook the fact that the design adaptations for meat-eating in the great cats are much more than just sharp teeth. A lion's finely programmed hunting instincts, immense muscular power capable of breaking a wildebeest's neck with one blow, and a digestive system (though it can cope with vegetables in a crisis) attuned to a diet of fresh meat make it overwhelmingly appear to be a highly designed hunting and killing machine. And such qualities are repeated in **millions** of instances. Before the Fall, what was the

function of the cheetah's blinding speed? What did the bombardier beetle use its highly complex twin cannons for (useful now to blast attackers) pre-Fall? If we could think of such a purpose, it would still leave open the question of how and when the programmed instincts to fire at beetle-eaters arose.

The idea that the snake's fangs may have been used to inject a fruit-softening substance pre-Fall has the same problem, of course. That is, why, how and when (if not by direct creation) did snakes all change not only their diet but their mode of life, which appears to be not a matter of conscious 'choice' so much as a program in their genetic code?[4]

In any case, the snake's venom contains complex chemicals which appear to be designed for purposes far removed from fruit-eating. One of these chemicals is highly specific in its attack on the central nervous system to arrest breathing; another specifically blocks the clotting mechanism so that the prey bleeds to death internally, and so on.

In spite of the above problems, this may still be the correct explanation in at least some, if not many, instances. The female mosquito does draw blood as it

needs haemoglobin for its reproductive processes. However, the male mosquito only sucks sap from plants. Perhaps both sexes drew sap from plants before the Fall, and with the eventual extinction of some plant species it was no longer possible to get haemoglobin from plants as easily (as mentioned previously, some living plants have haemoglobin).

POSITION No. 2

This essentially looks at complex design as requiring the direct hand of the Designer, whether for DAS or not. There are different possibilities within this, however. For example,

(i) There were no creatures with DAS pre-Fall — these creatures were all created afterwards.

The Bible makes no mention of such a creation. This would mean that most creatures alive today would not have had a pre-Fall representative. Not surprisingly, this is not widely held.

(ii) The design information for DAS was already present before the Fall, perhaps in latent or 'masked' form.

This implies that the Fall was foreknown by God, which of course reflects His omniscience, and also is clear in the assertion that Christ the Lamb was *'slain from the foundation of the world'* (Revelation 13:8). This information was allowed to come to expression, either through direct unmasking at the Fall, or through the natural processes of recombination and selection. If the latter was the case, this would again involve the foreknowledge of God, this time that there would be only a short time between creation and the Fall. Otherwise these DAS would come to the fore in Eden eventually. However, it is not easy to imagine genetically how such 'self-activation' could take place for such a vast number of creatures which must also interact ecologically (the appearance of a defence structure must take place very smartly after one's enemy has a 'new' weapon).

(iii) No new creatures were created, but many existing ones were 'redesigned' after the Fall, with the addition of new design information into their DNA. This position has only indirect Scriptural support, in that the serpent, at least, appears to have been radically and permanently redesigned by God at the Curse (Genesis 3:14). Perhaps Eve's body was likewise redesigned in relation to childbirth (Genesis 3:16). The ground is now to bring forth *'thorns and thistles'*; the sense seems to be that this will be the result of a sovereign directive as a result of Adam's sin, not something just being 'let go'.[5]

SUMMARY

Scripture simply does not provide enough information for Christians to be able to dogmatically insist that one or other of these possible explanations is totally right or wrong. Most probably a combination of several of them was operative. As fallen creatures in a fallen world, we will have difficulty imagining what a pre-Fall world was really like. We are also finite creatures lacking all the information. We therefore need to be particularly careful about arguing from the present to the past. What is clear from God's Word is that the present 'reign of tooth and claw', of violent death, cruelty and bloodshed, had no place in the world before Adam sinned.

APPENDIX
Population Explosion?

We see in today's post-Fall world that death, and animals eating others, is a useful way of avoiding overcrowding of the earth by any one type. Some therefore ask how, if there had been no Fall, such overcrowding could have been avoided without death and bloodshed.

In one sense, this may be a non-question, since Scripture indicates that Adam's rebellion (and thus the need for the shed blood of God's Lamb, Jesus Christ) was foreknown before the foundation of the world. However, even if this were not so, it is surely presumptuous to suggest that the all-powerful Creator would have been unable to devise other means of avoiding such a problem.

Interestingly, one such mechanism already exists and is well-known. Some animal populations studied, when subjected to overcrowding, drastically reduce their reproductive rate, only to increase it again if the population density should drop once more.

FOOTNOTES

1. Viruses, for instance, could have had a role pre-Fall in transferring genetic information. It would not take a major informational 'leap' upwards in complexity to enable them to cause disease instead. Mutation might indeed be capable of this.

2. This raises another problem — how much 'choice' can an animal be said to have in its way of life,

as opposed to programmed instinct? The only indirect scriptural support for this seems to be Genesis 6:7, 11–13 which has been understood to mean that the violence in the animal kingdom was one reason for the eradication of the land animals outside the Ark. However, this does not necessarily mean that God is attributing any moral responsibility to the animals — perhaps He is grieved because man's sin opened the door to the whole post-Fall reign of death and bloodshed.

3. This raises an old and interesting theological/philosophical question. Would God, being omnipotent, be any less responsible for DAS by having 'allowed' them to happen in some way than if He had actively designed them? An analogy is that of a doctor who, knowing that he could save a patient with the oxygen in his possession, fails to administer it. Is he less responsible than if he had actively killed the patient with cyanide? Some have pointed out that God is frequently actively involved in judgment without there being any ethical/theological dilemma — for instance, the sending of the great Flood which brought death and destruction to millions.

4. Another related issue is the presence in many animals of design features that are only useful in a post-Flood world — e.g. the anti-dehydration equipment of a camel, or the special insulating features of a polar bear's fur. Before the Flood, there probably were no deserts or polar ice caps. These design features were thus present in some form in the genetic information of their pre-Flood ancestors, unless one postulates that these features were specially created post-Flood, of which the Bible makes no mention.

5. In the future restoration, to get meat-eating lions (ML) to become grass-eating lions (GL) would seem to require supernatural rearranging of the DNA so as to make the change permanent for all future generations. Since ML — GL requires this, and since this is a 're'-storation (i.e. a reversal of the results of the Fall), perhaps this indicates that GL — ML happened by the same route (supernatural DNA reprogramming), only in the reverse direction.

7

Noah's Flood — where did the water go? (. . . and related matters)

IN telling us about the world-changing Flood in the days of Noah, the Bible gives us much information about where the waters came from and where they went.

The major source of the waters was 'the fountains of the great deep', which are mentioned first before the 'windows of heaven' in Genesis 7:11. They operated for 150 days during the Flood, whereas the rain lasted only 40 days and nights, there being a limit to the amount of water above the atmosphere (the 'windows of heaven').

These fountains were evidently created in the beginning to water the earth. We are told in Genesis 2:5–6 that there was no rain at first, but instead a mist went up from the earth to water the whole face of the ground. The Hebrew word here for mist not only suggests a mist or fog and its associated dew as we would understand this process today, but literal fountains, as geysers or springs. After all, there were four rivers that flowed from the Garden of Eden, and if there was no rain then such a spring would be the source of the water that then went in four directions as rivers through the garden. The importance of these fountains in the original created order is again emphasized in Revelation 14:7 where we are told that an angel will preach the everlasting Gospel with the words '. . . worship Him that made heaven, and earth, and the sea, and the fountains of waters.'

If the fountains of the deep were the major source of the waters, operating for the first 150 days of the Flood year, then they must have been a voluminous source of water. Some have suggested that when God made the dry land appear from underneath the waters on the third day of creation, then some of the water that covered the earth became trapped underneath and within the dry land. In any case, we are told in relation to the eruption of these fountains on the day the Flood began,

77

that there was a 'breaking up', which obviously implies large fissures in the ground. The waters that had been held under pressure inside the earth burst forth with catastrophic consequences. It is thus interesting to note that up to 90 per cent of what comes out of volcanoes even today is water, often in the form of steam. Because there are many volcanic rocks interspersed between the fossil layers in the rock record, layers that were obviously deposited during Noah's Flood, then it is quite appropriate to suggest that these fountains of the great deep may well

have involved a series of volcanic eruptions with prodigious amounts of water bursting up through the ground.

THE 'WINDOWS OF HEAVEN'

We are told that the other source of the waters for Noah's Flood was the opening of the 'windows of heaven'. We are then told that it rained for 40 days and 40 nights continually, implying that the opening of these windows meant the beginning of rainfall for the first time. We have already noted that Genesis 2:5 tells us that there was no rain at that former time. The implications of the Genesis account are that there was no rainfall until the time of the Flood, when these windows of heaven were opened and the rain fell. This would also explain why Noah preached for so long, with so few believing him, that it was going to rain. They had not experienced rain or local floods when Noah was preaching, and they scoffed at his warnings.

So what were these windows of heaven and why did it not rain for so long on the earth in those early days before the Flood? We are told in Genesis chapter 1 that on the second day of creation God divided the waters that were on the earth from the waters that He placed above the earth when he put a firmament or atmosphere in between those waters. It was into that atmosphere that He later placed the birds, so we know that this refers to the atmosphere that we breathe.

This means that there were waters **above** this atmosphere that are obviously not here today. This cannot refer to clouds, as they are **in** the atmosphere and produce rain. There was no rainbow either. We are told in Genesis 9:8–17 that God made a promise to Noah that He would never send a Flood like the one He had just sent, and that He put the rainbow in the sky as a sign of this covenant or promise. Specifically, God said (verse 13), *'I do set my bow in the cloud'* — a reference to the fact that one needs clouds to produce rainbows. The clouds are made up of water droplets. As the sun shines through those water droplets they act like glass prisms, so that the light is split up into its component colours and we see a rainbow. The whole thrust of this covenant is that this was a new thing that God was doing, so this was the first time the rainbow was seen.

So what were these waters above the atmosphere before the Flood? Many scholars regard these as water in vapour form that was held up by the atmosphere. The term normally used is 'water vapour canopy', implying a blanket of water vapour all the way around the earth. It is hard to imagine how liquid water could be suspended above the atmosphere, but water vapour would be much lighter than liquid water.

THE WATER VAPOUR CANOPY

Dr Joseph Dillow has calculated how much water vapour it would be physically possible to suspend above the atmosphere as a blanket around the earth.[1] He has suggested that it would be the water vapour equivalent of about 12 metres (40 feet) thickness of liquid water. He calculated that such a quantity of water would be sufficient to generate 40 days and 40 nights of torrential rainfall, whereas if these waters above had been clouds, then the moisture in the current atmosphere, if precipitated to earth as rainfall, would be only the equivalent of less than five centimetres (two inches) thickness of liquid water — hardly enough to sustain 40 days and 40 nights of rainfall at the time of the Flood.

Therefore it seems clear that the reference in Genesis 7:11 to the *'windows of heaven being opened'* is a reference to the collapse of this water vapour canopy, which somehow became unstable and fell as rain, the eyewitnesses describing the event as 'the windows of heaven being opened.' Some have suggested that when the fountains of the great deep broke open, presumably as volcanic eruptions, then the dust generated by these eruptions would have spread up into the water vapour canopy, causing the water vapour to nucleate with dust particles and form water droplets that then fell as rain.

There is other indirect evidence that is consistent with the existence of this water vapour canopy before the Flood. Such a canopy would have meant a very pleasant climate all around the globe at that time, since the earth's being encased in such a canopy would be akin to a glasshouse, where, much more than today, the heat of the sun's energy would be trapped inside the cocooning effect of the vapour canopy. Thus scholars talk of a 'greenhouse effect' before the Flood with a pleasant sub-tropical to temperate climate all around the globe, even at the poles where today there is ice. This would have meant the growth of lush vegetation on the land all around the globe. Evidence that this did happen in the past is the discovery of coal seams in Antarctica containing vegetation which is not now found growing at the poles, but which obviously grew under warmer conditions.

Such a lack of major temperature differences between poles and equator would mean that the major wind movements of today's world would not have taken place. We shall see later that the mountains were not as high before the Flood. In today's world, these major winds and high mountain ranges are a very

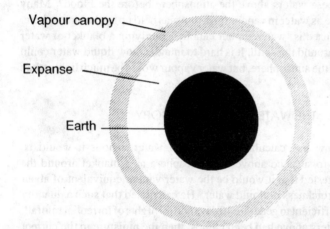

Vapour canopy

Expanse

Earth

Many scholars regard the 'waters above' as water in vapour form which was held up by the atmosphere.

important part of the cycle which brings rain on to the continents. Before the Flood, however, there was no need for either, because of the different way in which the earth was watered.

When we read the early chapters of Genesis, we also discover that the early patriarchs lived for very long ages — on average over 900 years. Many people find this unbelievable because today we live, on average, only 70 years. However, another implication of the water vapour canopy would be the protection of the inhabitants below from the incoming harmful cosmic radiation that may be partly responsible for the aging process. Others have suggested that a greater partial pressure of oxygen beneath such a canopy may also have increased the life-spans of men and animals. Air bubbles trapped in amber (fossilized tree resin) have shown a 50 per cent higher oxygen concentration than today. Thus the fact that the pre-Flood patriarchs lived to such long ages may be corroborative evidence for the existence of the water vapour canopy.

With the collapse of the water vapour canopy at the time of the Flood (the windows of heaven opening), it is not surprising to see that human life-spans became drastically reduced in the years following that event. Noah's immediate descendants lived substantially less than 900 years and within a few generations life-spans were reduced to the 70 years which humans on average now experience.

There are other startling implications of the existence of the water vapour canopy before the Flood, and the evidence for these is also corroborative evidence for its existence. Those interested in studying this issue further may consult Dr Joseph Dillow's book.[1]

WHERE DID THE WATERS GO?

So the whole earth was covered with the Flood waters, and the world that then existed was destroyed by the very waters out of which the earth had originally emerged at God's command (Genesis 1:9; 2 Peter 3:5–6). But where did those waters go afterwards?

There are a number of Scripture passages that identify the Flood waters with the present-day seas (Amos 9:6 and Job 38:8–11, note 'waves'). If the waters are

still here, how is it that the highest mountains are not still covered with water as they were in Noah's day? Psalm 104 gives us the answer. After the waters covered the mountains (verse 6), God rebuked them and they fled (verse 7); the mountains rose, the valleys sank down (verse 8) and God set a boundary so that they will never again cover the earth (verse 9). They are the same waters!

Isaiah gives this same statement that the waters of Noah should never again cover the earth (Isaiah 54:9). Clearly what the Bible is telling us is that God acted to alter the earth's topography. New continental land-masses bearing new mountain chains of folded rock strata were uplifted from below the globe-encircling waters that had eroded and levelled the pre-Flood topography, while large deep ocean basins were formed to receive and accommodate the Flood waters that then drained off the emerging continents.

That's why the oceans are so deep, and why there are folded mountain ranges. Indeed, if the entire earth's surface was levelled by smoothing out the topography of not only the land surface but also the rock surface on the ocean floor, then the waters of the ocean would cover the earth's surface to a depth of more than three kilometres (two miles). Quite clearly then, the waters of Noah's Flood are in today's ocean basins. We need to remember that nearly 70 per cent of the earth's surface is still covered by water.

A MECHANISM?

If at the close of the Flood the mountains rose while the valleys sank down, then such earth movements must have been primarily vertical in their operation, in marked contrast to the dominantly horizontal operation suggested by the theory of continental drift and plate tectonics proposed by most earth scientists today. In fact, there is a mechanism for vertical earth movements, one for which we have very good indirect evidence and some direct evidence (see Appendix I).

COULD THE WATER HAVE COVERED MOUNT EVEREST?

We have already suggested that the maximum height of the Flood waters over a theoretically level earth would have been about three kilometres (two miles). But Mt Everest, for instance, is more than eight kilometres (five miles) high. How, then, could the Flood have covered 'all the high hills under the whole heaven'? However, we have noted that very high mountains were not 'necessary' for rainfall in the pre-Flood world, and that the mountains today were formed **after** the Flood by this upthrusting mechanism. In support of this, one can observe that the layers which form the uppermost parts of Mt Everest are themselves composed of fossil-bearing, water-deposited layers.

Mt Everest — no mountains as high as this (eight kilometres, or five miles) before the Flood.

This process of uplift of the new continental land-masses from underneath the Flood waters would mean that, as the mountains rose and the valleys sank, the waters would rapidly drain off the newly emerging land surfaces. Such rapid movement of large volumes of water would cause erosion, and thus it is not hard to envisage the rapid carving out of many of the landscape features that we see on the earth today, including, for instance, places like the Grand Canyon of the USA, and Ayers Rock in central Australia. (The present shape of this monolith is the result of erosion following tilting and uplift of previously horizontal beds of water-laid sand.)

That is why we also see, in many cases, rivers in valleys today that are far larger than what should have been produced by the river, tiny by comparison, that now exists in them. In other words, the water flow responsible for carving out such large river valleys must have been greater than the volume of water flowing in the rivers today. This is consistent with the concept of voluminous Flood waters draining off the emerging land surfaces at the close of Noah's Flood and ending up in the rapidly sinking, newly prepared, deep ocean basins.

Appendix I
ISOSTASY

When allowances are made for altitude and centrifugal force, the earth appears to weigh much the same in different places. However, with the very sensitive gravity-measuring instruments developed in the past few years the earth can be weighed very accurately. Consequently, it has been found that the earth's apparent weight differs from one place to another, that is, gravity is marginally different. These differences seem to be due to the different densities of the rocks just below the instruments, because we know that the whole earth can have only one weight. Therefore, the differences must be caused by the different gravitational pulls of the rocks in the different parts of the crust.

For the ideal condition of gravitational equilibrium that controls the heights of continents and ocean floors, in accordance with the densities of the underlying rocks, the term isostasy (Greek for 'in equal-standing') was proposed by Dutton, an American geologist, in 1889.

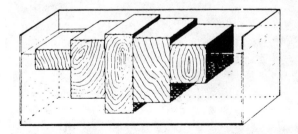

Wooden blocks of different heights floating in water (shown in front as a section through the tank), to illustrate the concept of isostatic balance between adjacent columns of the earth's crust.

The idea may be grasped by thinking of a series of wooden blocks of different heights floating in water (see diagram). The blocks emerge from the water by amounts which are proportional to their respective heights; they are said to be in a state of hydrostatic balance. Isostasy is the corresponding state of balance between extensive blocks of the earth's crust which rise to different levels and appear at the surface as mountain ranges, plateaus, plains or ocean floors.

Thus the earth's major relief is said to be compensated for by the underlying differences in rock density. Naturally, individual peaks and valleys are not separately balanced, since these minor relief features are easily maintained by the strength of the crustal rocks. None the less, the term isostasy expresses the idea that any two equal areas of the earth's crust, high or low, will weigh about the same. So where the crust is thin the rock material there should be more dense, and where the crust is thick, the rock material should be less dense.

These concepts have been confirmed by various evidence. For instance, gravity surveys made over the ocean gave the same result as those made on continents. The only explanation for this is to assume that according to isostasy the rocks beneath the ocean are more dense than those of the continents, because sea water is less dense than any rock. With the advent of techniques for sampling and even drilling into the rocks of the ocean floor, we have confirmed that the rocks there are denser than the average density of continental rocks.

Seismic studies, which have virtually enabled us to x-ray, as it were, the interior of the earth, have verified that the crust is thin and dense under the oceans, whereas the continental crust is much thicker and composed of less dense rocks. And now deep crustal drilling on the continents is confirming the thickness and density of the continental crust as indicated by the indirect evidence. It would appear, therefore, that the earth's crust is in approximate isostatic balance.

If material were removed from the continents by erosion, then the continents would become lighter in weight and tend to rise (just as a boat rises out of the water when its cargo is unloaded). Similarly, erosion mostly carries sediment seaward, so areas of heavy sedimentation such as deltas would become heavier and tend to sink.

Such processes were quite probably operative during the Flood year. The waters covered 'all the high hills under the whole of the heaven', so erosion would have devastated the pre-Flood geography. The earth's crust was likewise broken up to release the fountains of the great deep, no doubt accompanied by volcanic eruptions and the intrusion of igneous rocks. All in all, the isostatic balance of the pre-Flood crust would have been totally destroyed, so with the assuaging and retreating of the Flood waters a new isostatic balance would seek to establish itself. Perhaps this is one mechanism that might account for the vertical earth movements responsible for forming today's topography and height distribution during the closing stages of the Flood, as described in Psalm 104.

FOOTNOTE

1. Dillow, J., 1981. *The Waters Above*, Moody Press, Chicago.

8

How did all the different races arise (from Noah's family)?

ACCORDING to the Bible, all humans on earth today are descended from Noah and his wife, his three sons and their wives, and before that from Adam and Eve. It is obvious that we have many different groups or races with what seem to be greatly differing features. The most obvious of these is skin colour. Many see this as a reason to doubt the Bible's record of history. They believe that the various groups could have arisen only by evolving separately over tens of thousands of years.

As will be seen, this is not so. Modern knowledge of how features such as skin colour are inherited shows that it would have taken only a few generations after an event such as the Bible records as having happened at Babel to produce many different groups with distinct characteristics. And there is good evidence to show that in fact the various groups of people we have today have **not** been separated for huge periods of time.

WHAT IS A 'RACE'?

In one sense, of course, there is only one race — the human race. The Bible teaches us that God has *'made of one blood all nations of men'* (Acts 17:26). Scripture distinguishes people by tribal or national groupings, not by skin colour or physical appearances. Clearly, though, there are groups of people who have certain features (e.g. skin colour) in common, which makes them different from other groups. For convenience, we shall refer to these groups as races, since the human races are all part of one species — *Homo sapiens* ('wise man'). This, of course, tells us immediately that all races can freely interbreed and produce fertile offspring; if not, they would have to be classified as separate species. This indicates that the biological differences between the races are not very great.

Anthropologists generally classify people into a fairly small number of main racial groups, such as the Caucasoid, the Mongoloid (which includes for example the American Indians), the Negroid and the Australoid (the Australian Aborigines). Within each classification, there may be many different sub-groups.

Virtually all evolutionists would agree that the various races of men did not have separate origins — that is, they did not each evolve from a different group of animals, for instance. So they would agree with the biblical creationist that all races have come from the same original population. Of course, they believe that such groups as the Aborigines and the Chinese have had many, many tens of thousands of years of separation, and most people believe that there are such vast differences between the races that there **had** to be many years for these differences to somehow develop.

One reason for this is that people believe that some races have unique features

Virtually all evolutionists would agree with biblical creationists that all races have come from the same original population.

in their hereditary make-up which others do not. This is an understandable but incorrect idea. Let's look at skin colour, for instance. It is easy to think that since different groups of people have yellow skin, red skin, black skin, white skin and brown skin, then there must be many different skin pigments or colourings. And since different chemicals for colouring would mean a different genetic 'recipe' or code in the hereditary blueprint in each race, it appears to be a real problem. How could all those differences be present within a short time?

The **fact** is, however, that there is only **one** skin colour — melanin. This is a brownish pigment which we all have in special cells in our skin. If we have **none** (as do people called albinos, who suffer from an inherited mutation-caused defect, which means they lack the ability to produce melanin), then we will have a very white skin colouring (actually pink-white because of blood vessels showing through the skin). If we produce only a little melanin, it means that we will be 'European white'. If our skin produces a great deal of melanin, we will be a very deep black. And in between, of course, are all shades of brown. There are no other skin pigments; other factors such as the extra thickness of the overlying skin in the Chinese, for example, can give a yellowish effect. And this is not only true for skin colour — whatever feature we may look at, no race has anything which is, in its essence, uniquely different from that possessed by another. For example, the Chinese eye or almond eye gets its appearance simply by having an extra fold of fat (see Figure 1). Both Chinese and Caucasian eyes have fat — the latter simply have less of it.

We will shortly see how all the shades of skin colour would take only a very short time to come about, but first let's just find out what melanin is for. It protects the skin against the effects of sunlight. If you have too little in a very sunny environment, you will very easily suffer from sunburn and skin cancer. If you have a great deal of melanin, and you live in a country where

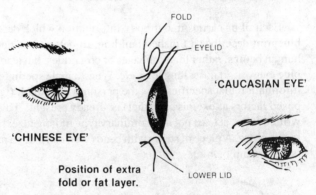

Fig. 1. *Both the Chinese eye and the Caucasian eye have fat. The Chinese eye simply has more of it.*

there is little sunshine, it is much harder for your body to get adequate amounts of vitamin D (which needs sunshine for its production in your body), and you may suffer from vitamin D deficiency which could cause a bone disorder such as rickets.

We also need to be aware that one is not born with a genetically fixed amount of melanin, but rather with a genetically fixed **potential** to produce a certain amount in response to sunlight. For example, if you are a Caucasian, you may have noticed that when your friends headed for the beach at the very beginning of summer, they may, if they spent all their time indoors during winter, have all been more or less the same pale white. As the summer went on, however, some became much darker than others. Even very dark-skinned races are not born with such a skin colour — it takes exposure to sunlight to 'switch on' the melanin 'factories' in the skin. In very dark-skinned people, the areas such as the palms of the hands and the soles of the feet, which are very rarely exposed to sunlight, generally stay much lighter than the rest of the body.

Let's look at a few observations which can help us to explain how many different skin colours can arise in a short time. (From here on, whenever we use such words as 'different colours' we are, strictly speaking, referring to different shades of the one colour.) If a person from a very black race marries someone from a very white race, their offspring (called 'mulattos') are mid-brown. It has long been known that if people of mulatto descent marry, their offspring may be virtually any colour, ranging from very black to very white. Understanding this gives us the clues we need for our overall question, so we must first look, in a simple way, at some of the basic facts of heredity.

HEREDITY

Each of us carries in our body information which describes us in the way a blueprint describes a finished building. It determines not only that we will be human beings, rather than cabbages or crocodiles, but also whether we will have blue eyes, short nose, long legs, etc. When a male sperm fertilizes an egg, **all** the information that specifies how the person will be built (ignoring such superimposed factors as exercise and diet) is already present. This information is not in written form, at least not in an ordinary type of language, but it is 'written down' in one sense. A piece of string with beads on it can carry a message in Morse code (see diagram below).

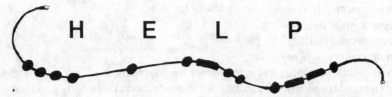

Can you see how the piece of string, by the use of a simple sequence of short beads, long beads, and spaces (to represent the dots and dashes of Morse code), can carry the same information as the English word 'help' typed on a sheet of paper? The entire *Encyclopaedia Britannica* could be 'written' thus in Morse Code on a long enough piece of string.

In a similar way, the human 'blueprint' is written in a code (or language convention) which is carried on a very long chemical called DNA.

The word 'gene' means a small part of that information which carries the instructions for only one feature. A small length of 'string' with only one 'specification' on it is a simple way of understanding it.

For example, there is one gene which carries the instructions on how to make haemoglobin, the chemical which carries oxygen in your red blood cells. If that gene has been damaged by mutation, the instructions will be faulty, so it will make a crippled form of haemoglobin, if any. (There are a number of diseases — e.g. sickle-cell anaemia, thalassaemia — which result from such mistakes, called mutations.)

So going back to that cell, that egg which has just been fertilized, where does all its information, its genes, come from? One half has come from the father (carried by the sperm) and the other half from the mother (carried in the egg). Genes come in matching pairs, so in the case of haemoglobin, for example, we have **two** genes which both contain the code (instruction) for haemoglobin manufacture, one from the mother and one from the father. This is a very useful arrangement, because if you inherit a gene from one parent which is damaged and can only instruct your cells to produce a defective haemoglobin, the other one from the other parent will continue to give the right instructions, so that only half the haemoglobin in your body is defective. (In fact, each of us carries hundreds of 'mistakes', inherited from one or the other of our parents, which are usefully 'covered up' by being matched with a normal gene from the other parent.)

Let's take another example, to ensure that before we talk about skin colour you will have a good basic understanding of heredity — simplified, of course. Blue and brown eyes are also a result of whether you have melanin in the iris of your eye. If you have it, your eyes are brown; if not, they appear blue, but they are, in fact, non-brown. (The sky appears blue, but has no blue colouring chemical in it.)

Let's call the gene which gives the instructions to make melanin in your iris 'B'. This gene says to your cells, in effect, 'Make melanin for the iris'. There is another gene[1] (let's call it 'b') which occupies the same place in the blueprint, and which 'says' nothing about manufacturing melanin. So if you inherit the 'B' from your father, and 'b' from your mother, they will line up together, as shown in Figure 2.

Figures 3 and 4 show what happens with different combinations.

Remember that a sperm from a man, or an egg from a woman, can carry only **one half** of any pair — if a man's code in relation to his eye colour is Bb, then his sperms can carry **either** b **or** B. So in Figure 5 we see how eye colour can be inherited:

Number 4 is the most interesting. Can you see how a child can be born with blue eyes although both parents have brown eyes? This is because both parents carried the 'hidden' factor for blue eyes. Continuing with Number 4, we can work out what proportion of their offspring, on average, should have blue eyes. We do this by means of a simple concept called a 'punnet square'. (Just persevere a little; it becomes relevant to skin colour in a moment!) (See Figure 6.)

The squares give you the possible combinations in the offspring; it is a little

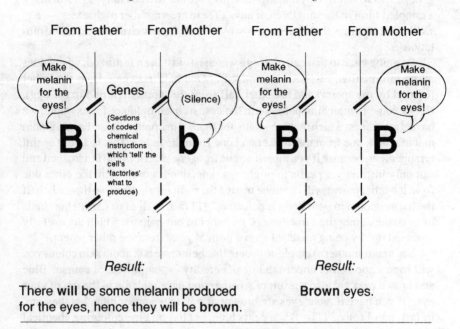

Fig. 2

From Father   From Mother

Make melanin for the eyes!

Genes

(Sections of coded chemical instructions which 'tell' the cell's 'factories' what to produce)

B

(Silence)

b

Result:

There will be some melanin produced for the eyes, hence they will be **brown**.

Fig. 3

From Father   From Mother

Make melanin for the eyes!

B

Make melanin for the eyes!

B

Result:

Brown eyes.

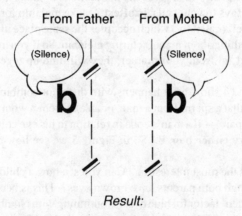

Fig. 4

From Father   From Mother

(Silence)

b

(Silence)

b

Result:

There is now **no** chemical instruction to make melanin for the eyes, so they will be **blue**.

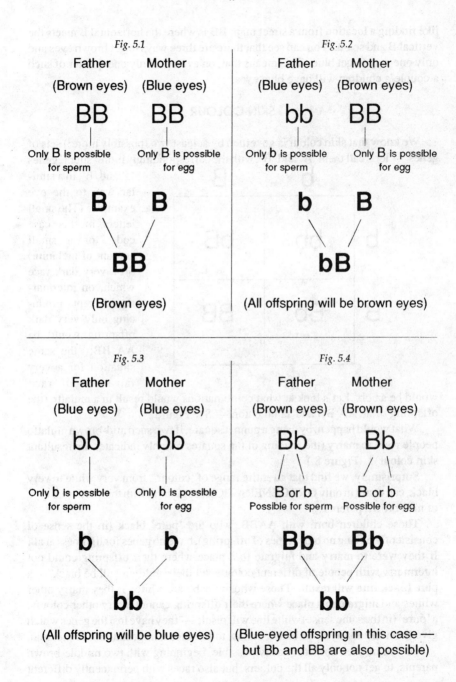

Fig. 5.1

Father (Brown eyes)   Mother (Blue eyes)

BB   BB

Only B is possible for sperm   Only B is possible for egg

B   B

BB

(Brown eyes)

Fig. 5.2

Father (Blue eyes)   Mother (Brown eyes)

bb   BB

Only b is possible for sperm   Only B is possible for egg

b   B

bB

(All offspring will be brown eyes)

Fig. 5.3

Father (Blue eyes)   Mother (Blue eyes)

bb   bb

Only b is possible for sperm   Only b is possible for egg

b   b

bb

(All offspring will be blue eyes)

Fig. 5.4

Father (Brown eyes)   Mother (Brown eyes)

Bb   Bb

B or b Possible for sperm   B or b Possible for egg

Bb   Bb

bb

(Blue-eyed offspring in this case — but Bb and BB are also possible) like finding a location from a street map; BB is where the horizontal B meets the vertical B and so on. You can see that there are three ways to get brown eyes and only one way to get blue. This means that, on average, only one quarter of such a couple's children will have blue eyes.

SKIN COLOUR

We know that skin colour is governed by at least two (possibly more[2]) sets of genes — let's call them 'A' and 'B', with the correspondingly more 'silent' genes

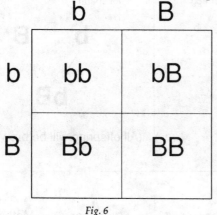

'a' and 'b', in a similar way to the eye example. (The small letters in this case code for a small amount of melanin.) So a very dark race which, on intermarriage, kept producing only very dark offspring would be AA BB; the same situation for a very fair-skinned race

Fig. 6

would be aa bb. Let's look at what combinations would result in a mulatto (the offspring of an AA BB and aa bb union — See Figure 7.)

What would happen, by using a punnet square, if two such mid-brown mulatto people were to marry (the shading of the squares roughly indicates the resultant skin colour)? (Figure 8.)

Surprisingly, we find that an entire range of 'colour', from very white to very black, can result in only ONE GENERATION, beginning with this particular type of mid-brown parents.

Those children born with AABB, who are 'pure' black (in the sense of consistently having no other types of offspring), have no genes for lightness at all. If they were to marry and migrate to a place where their offspring could not intermarry with people of different colours, all their children will be black — a pure **black line** will result. Those who are aabb are white; if they marry other whites and migrate to a place where their offspring cannot marry other colours, a 'pure' (in the same sense) white line will result — they have lost the genes which give them the ability to be black, that is, to produce a large amount of melanin.

So you can see how it is easily possible, beginning with two middle-brown parents, to get not only all the colours, but also races with permanently different shades of colouring. But what about races which are permanently middle-brown, such as we have today? Again, this is easily explained. Those of aaBB or AAbb, if they no longer interact with others, will be able to produce only mid-brown coloured offspring. (You may want to work this out with your own punnet square.)

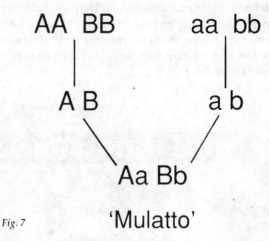

Fig. 7

If these 'pure' lines were to interbreed again with other such lines, the process would be reversed. In a short time, their descendants would show a whole range

MAXIMUM VARIATION
AaBb x AaBb

Fig. 8

We all have the same basic skin colour agent, melanin, but in varying amounts. Parents with genes that code only for dark colours (AABB) will have only dark children. Parents with only light skin (aabb) will have only light-skinned children.

	AB	Ab	aB	ab
AB	AA BB	AA Bb	Aa BB	Aa Bb
Ab	AA Bb	AA bb	Aa Bb	Aa bb
aB	Aa BB	Aa Bb	aa BB	aa Bb
ab	Aa Bb	Aa bb	aa Bb	aa bb

ONLY DARK AABB

ONLY MEDIUM AAbb OR aaBB

ONLY LIGHT aabb

of colours, often in the same family. The photo in Figure 9 shows what were called 'Britain's most amazing twins'. One is obviously white, the other obviously dark-skinned. Of course, this is not amazing at all when you do the exercise on paper, based on what we have discussed. (A clue if you want to do it yourself — mother cannot be AABB.)

PERTH SATURDAY AUGUST 20 1983
Telephone 321 0161 (Classified 420 1111)

MIXED DOUBLES

Two-tone twins Meet Britain's most amazing twins — in black and white. Thomas is black and Wesley is white. The brothers, now 17-months-old, were born in Lancashire to Mandy and Tom Charnock. Mrs Charnock is part-Nigerian — her mother is English and her father is Nigerian — while her husband Tom is English. Their story is told in **Page 5** today.

Fig. 9.
A fascinating mix of genes. Mandy and Tom Charnock gave birth to twins — one white, one black.

If all the humans on earth were to intermarry freely, then break into random groups which kept to themselves, a whole new set of combinations could emerge. It may be possible to have almond eye with black skin, blue eyes with black frizzy short hair, etc. We need to remember, of course, that the way in which genes express themselves is turning out to be much more complex than this simplified picture. Sometimes certain genes are linked together. However, the basic point is unaffected.

Even today, close observation shows that within a particular race you will often see a feature normally associated with another. For instance, you will occasionally see a European with a broad flat nose, or a Chinese with very pale skin.

Geneticists who study other, less obvious, characteristics are now aware that the difference between the average of each race is not as great as the existing variation within each race. This also argues strongly against the idea that the races have been evolving separately for long periods.

WHAT REALLY HAPPENED?

We can now reconstruct the true history of the races, using:
● The background information given above.
● The information given by the Creator Himself in the book of Genesis.
● Some consideration of the effect of the environment.

The first created man, Adam, from whom all other humans are descended, was created with the best possible combination of genes — for skin colour, for example. A considerable time after creation a world-wide flood destroyed all humans except a man called Noah, his wife, his three sons and their wives. This flood greatly changed the environment. Afterwards, God commanded the survivors to multiply and cover the earth. A few hundred years later, men had chosen to disobey God and to remain united in building a great city, with the Tower of Babel as the focal point of rebellious worship. From Genesis 11 we understand that up to this time there was only one language, and that God judged the people's disobedience by imposing different languages on man, so that they could not work together against God, and so that they were forced to scatter over the earth as God had originally intended.

So all the races — the Negro, the European, the Australian Aboriginal, and the others, have come into existence since that time.

Noah and his family were probably mid-brown, with genes for both dark and light skin, because a medium skin colour (dark enough to protect against skin cancer, yet light enough to allow vitamin D production) would be the most suitable in the world before the Flood. (It is likely that there were then no harsh extremes of climate.) As all the factors for skin colour were present in Adam and Eve they would most likely have been mid-brown as well. In fact, most of the world's population today is still mid-brown in colour.

After the Flood, for the few centuries till Babel, there was only one language and one culture group. Thus there were no barriers to marriage within this group. This would tend to keep the skin colour of the population away from the extremes. Very dark and very light skin would appear, of course, but people tending in either direction would be free to marry someone less dark or less light than themselves, ensuring that the average colour stayed roughly the same. The same would be true of other characteristics, not just skin colour. Under these sorts of circumstances, distinct racial lines will never emerge. This is true for animals as well as human populations, as every biologist knows. To obtain such separate lines, you would need to break a large breeding group into smaller groups and keep them separate — that is, not interbreeding any more.

THE EFFECTS OF BABEL

This is exactly what happened at Babel. Once separate languages were imposed, there were instantaneous barriers. Not only would people tend not to marry someone they couldn't understand, but entire groups which spoke the same language would have difficulty relating to and trusting those which did not. They would tend to move away or be forced away from each other, into different environments. This, of course, is what God intended. It is unlikely that each small group would carry the same broad range of skin colours as the original, larger group. So one group might have more 'dark' genes, on average, while another might have more 'light' genes. The same thing would happen to other characteristics — nose shape, eye shape, etc. And since they would interbreed only within their own language group, this tendency would no longer be 'averaged out' as before.

As these groups migrated away from Babel, they encountered new and different climate zones. This would also have affected the balance of inherited factors in the population, although the effects of the environment are nowhere near as important as the genetic 'mix' with which each group began. As an example, let us look at people who moved to cold areas with little sunlight. In those areas, the dark-skinned members of any group would not be able to produce enough vitamin D and thus would be less healthy and have fewer children. So in time, the light-skinned members would predominate. If several different groups went to such an area, and if one group happened to be carrying few genes for lightness, this particular group could in time die out. This natural selection acts on the characteristics already present, and does not evolve new ones.

It is interesting to note that in the Neanderthals of Europe, an extinct race of men (now recognized as fully human), virtually all showed evidence of vitamin D deficiency in their bony skeletons. In fact, it was this, plus a large dose of evolutionary prejudice, which helped cause them to be classified as 'ape-men' for a long time. It is thus quite plausible to suggest that they were a dark-skinned race who were 'unfit' for the environment into which they moved because of the skin colour genes **they began with**. (Notice that this 'natural selection', as it is called, does not **produce** skin colours, but only acts on the created colours that are already there.)

Conversely, fair-skinned people in very sunny regions could easily be affected by skin cancer, in which case dark-skinned people would more readily survive.

So we see that the pressure of the environment can (a) affect the balance of genes within a group, and (b) even eliminate entire groups. This is why we see, to a large extent, a 'fit' of characters to their environment (e.g. Nordic people with pale skin, equatorial people with dark skin).

But this is not always so. The Eskimo has darkish skin yet lives where there is not much sun. The pygmy is in a hot area, but rarely experiences sunshine in his dense jungle environment. And pygmies may be a good example of another factor which has affected the racial history of man — discrimination. If a variation from the normal occurs (e.g. a very light person in a dark race), then

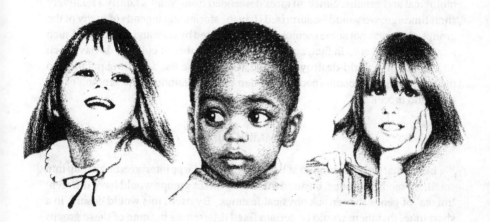

historically it has been usual for that person to be regarded as abnormal and unacceptable. Thus such a person would find it hard to get a marriage partner. This would further tend to eliminate 'light' genes from a dark race, and vice versa. In this way, groups have tended to 'purify' themselves. Also, in some instances, interbreeding in a small group can highlight any commonly occurring unusual features which would previously have been 'swamped' by continual intermarriage. There is a tribe in Africa whose members all have grossly deformed feet as a result of this inbreeding.

To return to pygmies, if people possessing genes for such short stature were discriminated against because of their size, and a small group of them sought refuge in the deepest forest, their marrying only each other would ensure a 'pygmy' race from then on. The fact that pygmy tribes never have their own languages, but instead speak dialects of neighbouring non-pygmy tribal languages, is good evidence in support of this.

THE EFFECTS OF CHOICE

Human groups that were already equipped with certain characteristics may have made deliberate (or semi-deliberate) choices concerning the environments to which they migrated. For instance, people with genes for a thicker, more insulating layer of fat under their skin would tend to leave areas that were uncomfortably hot.

OTHER EVIDENCE

The evidence for the Bible's account of human origins is more than just biological and genetic. Since all races descended from Noah's family a relatively short time ago, we would be surprised if, in the stories and legends of many of the groups, there was not some memory, albeit distorted by time and retelling, of such a catastrophic event. In fact, an overwhelming number of cultures do have such an account of a world-destroying Flood. Often these have startling parallels to the true, original account (people saved in a boat, a rainbow, the sending of the birds and more).

SUMMING UP

In summary, the dispersion at Babel, breaking a large interbreeding group into small, inbreeding groups, ensured that the resultant groups would have different 'mixes' of genes for various physical features. By itself, this would ensure, in a short time, that there would be certain fixed differences in some of these groups which we would call separate 'races'. In addition, the selection pressure of the environment would modify the existing combinations of genes, causing a tendency for characteristics to suit their environment. There has been no simple-to-complex evolution of any genes, for the genes were present already. The features of the various races result from different combinations of previously existing created genes, plus some minor changes in the direction of degeneration, resulting from mutation (accidental changes which can be inherited). The originally created (genetic) information has been either reshuffled or degenerated, not added to.

CONSEQUENCES OF A FALSE BELIEF
CONCERNING THE ORIGIN OF THE RACES

● **Rejection of the Gospel**
Since the accuracy of the historical details of Genesis is crucial to the trustworthiness of the Bible, and to the whole Gospel message,[3] the popular belief that races have 'evolved' their different features, and could not all have come from Noah's family, has eroded belief in the Gospel of Jesus Christ.

● **Racism**

One of the biggest justifications for racial discrimination in modern times is the belief that, because races have allegedly evolved separately, they are at different stages of evolution and some races are more backward. Thus the other person's race may not be as fully human as your own.

● **Influence on Missionary Outreach**

Historically, the spread of evolutionary belief was associated with a slackening of fervour to reach the lost in far-away countries. The idea of savage, half-evolved inferior peoples somehow does not give rise to the same missionary urgency as the notion that our 'cousins', closely linked to us in time and heredity, have yet to hear the Gospel. Even many of the finest of today's missionary organizations have been influenced, often unconsciously, by this deeply ingrained belief in the evolutionary view of how other peoples and their religions came about.

The Bible makes it clear that any newly 'discovered' tribe is not a group of people who have never had any superior technology or knowledge of God in their culture. Rather, their culture began with (a) a knowledge of God, and (b) technology at least sufficient to build a boat of ocean-liner size. In looking for the reasons for some of this technological loss and cultural degeneration (see Appendix II), Romans 1 suggests that it is linked to the deliberate rejection by one of their ancestors of the worship of the living God. A full appreciation of this would mean that we would not see the need to educate several generations and give them technical aid as a first priority, but would see their real and urgent need for the Gospel as first and foremost.

In fact, most 'primitive' tribes still have a memory, in their folklore and religion, of the fact that their ancestors turned away from the living God, the Creator. Don Richardson, missionary of *Peace Child* fame, has shown that a missionary approach unblinded by evolutionary bias, and thus looking for this link and utilizing it, has borne a bountiful and blessed harvest on many occasions.[4]

Jesus Christ, God's reconciliation in the face of man's rejection of the Creator, is the truth that can set men and women of **every** culture, technology, race or colour, truly free.

APPENDIX I
Black people and the curse on Ham.

The above shows clearly that the 'blackness' of, for example, Negroes, is merely one particular combination of inherited factors. This means that these factors themselves, though not in that combination, were originally present in Adam and Eve. Black skin could not, therefore, have come about from the curse on Ham. This common belief that the skin colour of black people is a result of a curse on Ham and his descendants is nowhere taught in the Bible. It has been used to justify slavery and other non-biblical racist attitudes. It is traditionally believed that the African nations are largely

Hamitic, and there is some evidence for this. Genesis suggests that the dispersion was probably along family lines, and it may be that Ham's descendants were on average darker than, say Japheth's. However, it could just as easily have been the other way around.

APPENDIX II
'Stone Age' people

Archaeology shows that there were once people who lived in caves and used simple stone tools. Observation shows that there are still people who do the same. We have seen evidence that all people on earth today are descended from Noah and his family. Before the Flood, Genesis indicates, there was at least sufficient technology to make musical instruments, to farm, build cities and build a very large seaworthy vessel. After the dispersion at Babel, the hostilities induced by the new languages may have forced some groups to scatter rather rapidly, finding shelter where and when they could.

In some instances, the stone tools may simply have been a stage until their settlements were fully established and they had found and exploited metal deposits, for example. In others, the original diverging group may not have taken all the knowledge with them. Ask an average group today how many of them, if they had to 'start again' as it were, would know how to find, mine and smelt metal-bearing rocks (orebodies)? Obviously, there has been technological degeneration.

In some cases, harsh environments may have contributed. The Australian Aborigines have a technology and cultural knowledge which, in relation to their lifestyle and need to survive in the dry outback, is most appropriate. This included aerodynamic principles used in making boomerangs, some of which were designed to return to the thrower; others were not.

Sometimes we see evidence of degeneration which is hard to explain, but is real none the less. For instance, when Europeans arrived in Tasmania, the Aborigines there had the simplest technology known. They caught no fish, and did not know how to make fire. Yet recent archaeological discoveries lead us to infer that some generations earlier they had more knowledge and equipment.

For instance, archaeologist Rhys Jones believes that in the Aborigines' distant past, these people had equipment to sew skins into more complex clothes than the skins they just slung over their shoulders according to all descriptions in the early 1800s. It also appears that they were in fact catching and eating fish in the past, but when white men arrived, they had not been doing this for a long time.[5,6] From this we infer that technology can indeed be lost or abandoned, and is not always retained and built upon.

FOOTNOTES

1. Actually the technical term for varying forms of the same gene is an 'allele', but that is not important here.
2. There are thought to be four, in actual fact, which does not detract from the argument using two as a useful example, and makes for a greater range of skin shading.
3. Ham, Ken, 1987, *The Lie: Evolution*, Creation-Life Publishers, San Diego, California, USA.
4. Richardson, Donald, 1986, *Eternity in Their Hearts*, Regal Books, Division of Gospel Light, Ventura, California, USA.
5. Jones, R., 1987. Tasmania's Ice-Age hunters. *Australian Geographic*, No. 8, (Oct.–Dec.), pp. 26–45.
6. Jones, R., 1977. The Tasmanian paradox. In: Wright, R. S. V. (Editor), *Stone Tools as Cultural Markers*, Australian Institute of Aboriginal Studies, Canberra.

9

What about the 'Gap' theory (or 'ruin-reconstruction' theory)?

Part A — Problems and Inconsistencies

'THEISTIC evolution' and 'progressive creation' are among the many attempts made to harmonize the Genesis account of Creation with accepted 'modern' geology. The 'gap' theory[1] was another significant attempt by Christian theologians to reconcile the apparently short scale of world history found in Genesis with the popular belief that geologists provide 'undeniable' evidence that the world is exceedingly old (currently estimated at about 4.7 billion years).

Thomas Chalmers (1780–1847), a notable Scottish theologian and first Moderator of the Free Church of Scotland, was perhaps the man most responsible for the origin and popularity of the 'gap' theory.[2]

Basically, the 'gap' theory incorporates three strands of thought:
1. Belief in a literal view of Genesis.
2. Belief in an extremely long but undefined age for the earth.
3. An obligation to fit the origin of most of the geologic strata and other geologic evidence between Genesis 1:1 and 1:2. 'Gap' theorists are opposed to evolution, but do not believe in a recent origin of the universe.

According to Fields,[3] the theory can be summarized as follows:

'In the far distant dateless, past God created a perfect heaven and perfect earth. Satan was ruler of the earth which was peopled by a race of "men" without any souls. Eventually, Satan, who dwelled in a garden of Eden composed of minerals

(Ezek. 28), rebelled by desiring to become like God (Isa. 14). Because of Satan's fall, sin entered the universe and brought on the earth God's judgment in the form of a flood (indicated by the water of 1:2), and then a global ice-age when the light and heat from the sun were somehow removed. All the plant, animal, and human fossils upon the earth today date from this "Lucifer's flood" and do not bear any genetic relationship with the plants, animals and fossils living upon the earth today.'

This period supposedly fits between Genesis 1:1 and 1:2.

Western Bible commentaries written before the eighteenth century, and before the belief in a long age for the earth became popular, proposed no gap between Genesis 1:1 and Genesis 1:2. Certainly some commentaries proposed intervals of various lengths of time for reasons relating to Satan's fall, but none ever proposed a 'ruin-reconstruction' situation, or pre-Adamite world. In the eighteenth century, it became popular to believe that geological changes occurred slowly, and roughly at the present rate (uniformitarianism[4]).

With this increased acceptance of uniformitarianism, many theologians urged reinterpretation of Genesis (see Diagram 1).

PROBLEMS

The following are some of the difficulties and inconsistencies confronting those who adhere to the 'gap' theory:

● 'Gap' theorists accept that the earth is very old. They base this view on the acceptance of geologic evidence using the assumption that the present is the key to the past. This assumption implies that in the past, sediments containing fossils formed at basically the same rate as they do today. It is also used by most geologists and biologists to seek to justify belief in the geologic column, that is, the total picture of world history preserved in the rocks (see Diagram 2). This geologic column has become the showcase of evolution because the fossils are interpreted as showing 'ascent' from simple to complex forms. This places the 'gap' theorist in a dilemma. He is committed to literal creation because of his acceptance of a 'literal view' of Genesis, yet he cannot accept the conclusions of evolution based on the geologic column. Nor can he accept that the days in the Genesis record correspond to geologic periods. He therefore proposes that God reshaped the earth and re-created all life in six literal days after 'Lucifer's Flood' (which produced the fossils); hence the name 'ruin-reconstruction'. This flood was supposedly caused by the sin of Satan, and the resulting judgment upon that sin reduced the previous world to a state 'without form and void.'

Now while the 'gap' theorist may think he has solved the problem, his solution (Lucifer's Flood) in reality has removed the reason for which he proposed the

INTERPRETATIONS OF GENESIS (WESTERN EUROPE 1400–PRESENT)

FLOOD GEOLOGY	BIBLICAL INTERPRETATION	MODERN GEOLOGY
1400 — Catastrophic geology popular — most sediments and fossils believed to be evidence of Noah's Flood	Creation in Genesis accepted at literal face value	
1700		Popularization of belief in uniformitarianism, led to popular belief in long time-scale for the sediments
1750 — Catastrophic belief led to short time-scale for sediments **i.e. YOUNG EARTH**	**CONFLICT!**	**i.e. OLD EARTH**
1770 — Catastrophic geology diminishes in popularity	Adherence to literal creation Reinterpretation of Genesis 'Christian Agnostics'	Sediments now arranged on basis that simplest fossils found in oldest rocks
	Gap Theory Day-age Theory	
1859	Theistic evolution	Darwin popularizes evolution, Huxley promotes it
		Order of fossils in rocks used as key proof for evolution
1907		Radiometric dating invoked as absolute proof of old earth
1920 — Re-emergence of flood geology	**CONFLICT!**	Uniformitarian geology now under attack but still dominant assumption of modern geology.
1980 — Re-popularization of flood geology among educated Protestants	Literal Day-age Agnostic Gap Theistic Evolution	

Diagram 1

theory in the first place (the supposed vast age of the earth). If all, or most, of the sediments and fossils were produced quickly in one massive world-wide Lucifer's Flood, then the evidence that the earth is extremely old (based on the slow formation of the sediments) no longer exists. If the world was reduced to a shapeless chaotic mass, 'without form and void', how could an ordered assemblage of fossils and sediments remain as evidence? Surely with such chaos the fossil record would have been severely disrupted, if not entirely destroyed.

● If the fossil record is explained on the basis of Lucifer's Flood, then what effect did the world-wide Flood of Noah have? On this point the 'gap' theorist is forced to conclude that Noah's Flood must have left virtually no trace. Genesis, however, depicts Noah's Flood as a judgment for man's sins (Genesis 6). Water covered the whole world for more than a year (Genesis 6:17 and 7:19–24). Only one family survived (Genesis 7:23b). Plants and all life that had breath, died. One can understand the 'gap' theorist's difficulty in maintaining a literal acceptance of Genesis including the catastrophic Noah's Flood, while not allowing for any trace of that event. Some 'gap' theorists overcome this problem by suggesting that Noah's Flood was local.

● The true 'gap' theorist also ignores any evidence consistent with a belief in a young age for the earth of possibly no more than 10,000 years. But there is much evidence for this — the decay of the earth's magnetic field, the quantity of helium in the earth's atmosphere, and the break-up of galaxy clusters.[5]

● Exodus 20:11 states, '*For in six days the Lord made heaven and earth, the sea, and all that in them is, and rested the seventh day: wherefore the Lord blessed the Sabbath day, and hallowed it.*' Thus the creation of the heavens and the earth (Genesis 1:1) and the sea and **all** that is in them (the rest of the Creation) was completed in six days. Where is there time for a gap? If you accept that the geologic column was in existence before Adam (as does the 'gap' theorist), then God must have made the fossil-containing strata during the six days, for there was no room for a gap.

● On the basis of Romans 5:12, '*Wherefore, as by one man [Adam] sin entered into the world, and death by sin; and so death passed upon all men, for that all have sinned*', it is understood that there could not have been human sin or death before Adam. The Bible teaches (1 Corinthians 15) that not only was Adam the first man, but as a result of his rebellion (sin) death and corruption entered the universe. Before Adam sinned there could not have been any animal or human death. Note also that there could not have been a race of men before Adam that died in Lucifer's Flood. Genesis 1:29 and 30 teach us that the animals and man were originally created vegetarian. This is consistent with God's description of the Creation as 'very good'. How could a fossil record which gives evidence of disease, violence, death and decay (fossils

Geologic Column

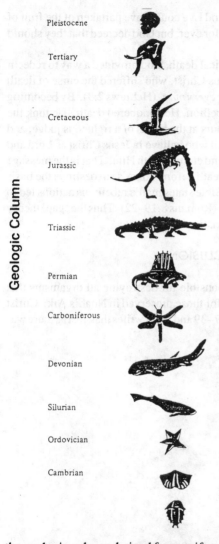

Pleistocene

Tertiary

Cretaceous

Jurassic

Triassic

Permian

Carboniferous

Devonian

Silurian

Ordovician

Cambrian

have been found of animals apparently fighting and certainly eating each other) be described as 'very good'? Thus, the death of billions of animals (including many humans) as seen in the fossil record must be explained as occurring after Adam's sin. The historical event of Noah's Flood, recorded in Genesis, provides the means to explain the dead animals buried in rock layers laid down by water all over the earth.

Romans 8:22 teaches that *'we know that the whole creation groaneth and travaileth in pain together until now.'* Clearly the whole of creation was, and is, subject to decay and corruption because of sin. The fossil record shows disease, decay and death. When the 'gap' theorist believes that disease, decay and death existed before Adam sinned, he ignores that this is contrary to the teaching of Scripture.

Moreover, the 'gap' theory fails to satisfy evolutionary or uniformitarian science as its advocates hoped it would. By accepting an ancient age for the earth (based on the geologic column derived from uniformitarian geology), 'gap' theorists leave the evolutionary system intact (which by their own assumptions they oppose). Even worse, they must also theorize that Romans 5:12 and Genesis 3:3 refer only to spiritual death. This is not borne out by Scripture. (See 1 Corinthians 15; Genesis 3:22–23.) These passages conclude that Adam's sin led to physical death as well as spiritual death. In 1 Corinthians 15 the death of the last Adam (the Lord Jesus Christ) is compared to the death of the first Adam. Jesus suffered physical death for man's sin, and Adam, the first man, died physically because of sin.

Genesis 3:22–23 tells us that if Adam and Eve could have partaken of the fruit of the Tree of Life, they would have lived for ever, but God decreed that they should die physically because of their sin.

In placing on man the curse of physical death, God provided a way to redeem man through the person of His Son Jesus Christ, who suffered the curse of death on the cross for us. *'He tasted death for every man'* (Hebrews 2:9). By becoming the perfect sacrifice for our sin and rebellion, He conquered death. He took the penalty that should rightly have been ours at the hands of a righteous judge, and bore it in His own body on the cross. All who believe in Jesus Christ as Lord and Saviour are received back to God to spend eternity with Him. That is the message of Christianity. To believe there was death before Adam's sin destroys the basis of the Christian message, because the Bible states man's rebellious actions led to death and the corruption of the universe (Romans 8:19–22). Thus the 'gap' theory undermines the foundations of the Christian message.

CONCLUSION

Genesis records a catastrophe responsible for destroying all organisms that had the 'breath of life in them' except for those preserved in Noah's Ark. Christ refers to Noah's Flood in Matthew 24:37–39 and Peter writes that, just as there was

once a world-wide judgment of mankind by water, so there will be another world-wide judgment, next time by fire (2 Peter 3).

Isn't it more consistent with the whole framework of Scripture to correlate most fossil deposits with Noah's Flood, than to resort to the fall of Satan (a vague

area of Scripture) to justify a speculative geological catastrophe which achieves nothing for biblical understanding or science?

Moreover, to advocate death before Adam sinned is diametrically opposed to Scripture's explanation that death came only after Adam sinned, which then brought the necessity for man's redemption.

Rather than accept God's Word by faith, many sincere Christians have sought to avoid intellectual conflicts with scientific ideas. The 'gap' theory was one such re-interpretation of Scripture designed to fit in with the favoured scientific concepts of the day.

Part B — A Closer
Look at Genesis 1:1–2

INTRODUCTION

The 'ruin-reconstruction' interpretation of Genesis 1 emerged about the end of the eighteenth century, first in response to demands by geological science for vast periods of time to permit the slow laying down of the strata, and second, in order to account for the alleged great antiquity of the fossils.

The earliest available translation of Genesis 1:1–2 is found in the Greek translation of the Old Testament, prepared during the century following 250–200 BC. The Septuagint, or LXX, does not permit the reading of any 'Ruin-Reconstruction' scenario into these verses, as even Arthur Custance (a leading defender of the 'gap' theory) admits. A closer look at the interpretation of these verses reveals that the 'gap' theory imposes an interpretation upon Genesis 1:1–2 which is unnatural, and grammatically unsound. Like many attempts to harmonize the Bible with science, the 'gap' theory involves a well-meant but misguided twisting of Scripture.

In the following discussion we will consider the four major issues of interpretation bearing on the 'gap' theory. For a much fuller analysis, the reader is strongly advised to study the book *Unformed and Unfilled*.[6]

CREATING AND MAKING
(HEBREW: *bârâ'* and *'âsâh*)

It is generally acknowledged that the Hebrew word *bârâ'*, used with 'God' as its subject, means 'to create'. In the words of Keil, it refers to 'the production of

An argument for the 'gap' theory is that the Hebrew words for 'created' and 'made' always have different meanings. In fact, they are used interchangeably in certain contexts.

that which had no existence before.'

However, faced with God's statement in the Fourth Commandment that He 'made' (*'âsâh*) the heavens and earth in six days (Exodus 20:11), 'gap' theorists (or 'gappists') have alleged that *'âsâh* cannot mean 'to create'. They say that Exodus 20:11 refers not to six days of creation, but six days of re-forming a ruined world.

Is there such a difference between *bârâ'* and *'âsâh* in biblical usage?

A number of verses show that while *'âsâh* may mean 'to do', 'to make', it may also bear the meaning 'to create', the same as *bârâ'*. For example, Nehemiah 9:6 states that God made (*'âsâh*) *'the heavens, even the highest heavens, and all their starry host, the earth and all that is on it, the seas and all that is in them'* (NIV).

The reference is obviously to the original *ex nihilo* creation, but the word *'âsâh* is used. (We may safely presume that no 'gappist' will want to say that Nehemiah 9:6 refers to the supposed 'reconstruction', because if it did, the 'gappist' would have to include the ordered strata of geology as well, thereby depriving his whole theory of any purpose!)

The fact is that the two words *bârâ'* and *'âsâh* may often be used interchangeably in the Old Testament; indeed, in some places they are used in synonymous parallelism (e.g. Genesis 2:4; Exodus 34:10; Isaiah 41: 20; 43:7). Applying this conclusion to Exodus 20:11 (cf. 31:17) as well as Nehemiah 9:6, we see that Scripture teaches that God created the universe in six days, as outlined in Genesis chapter 1.

THE GRAMMAR OF GENESIS 1:1–2

Many adherents of the 'gap' theory affirm that the grammar of Genesis 1:1–2 allows, and even requires, a time-gap between what is recorded in verse 1, and what is said in verse 2. Into this gap — believed by many to be millions of years —they wish to place all the major geological phenomena which have shaped the world. This interpretation gained wide publicity through the footnotes to the first *Scofield Reference Bible* (1909), but the initial impetus had come 100 years before by its being espoused by the renowned Dr Thomas Chalmers, who became first Moderator of the Free Church of Scotland in 1843.

Let us look at these verses. The first thing to say is that this is a most unnatural interpretation: it is not what lies on the surface of the text. The most straightforward reading of the verses sees verse 1 as a subject-and-verb clause,

THE 'GAP' THEORY

'GAP' THEORY	EVOLUTIONARY BELIEF
Accepts the geologic record and explains it by a hypothetical catastrophe (Lucifer's Flood).	
As most geologic strata are explained on the basis of Lucifer's Flood, no geologic model can be built up from Noah's Flood, that is, Noah's Flood produced no fossils, etc.	Geologic column built up on the basis of uniformitarian processes: little or no catastrophism.
The earth became 'formless and void' after the catastrophe (Lucifer's Flood) formed most of the fossil record.	Little or no catastrophism allowed (some recent changes to this, but definitely no world-wide catastrophism).
There had to be death and sin before Adam, as the whole 'pre-Adamite' world perished (a judgment) in Lucifer's Flood.	Death is a necessary part of the evolutionary system: evolution requires death.
There was a race of men without souls on the world before Adam. This race was destroyed by Lucifer's Flood.	Man evolved from ape-like creatures one–three million years ago.
The fossil men in the fossil record are the remains of the soulless men from the 'pre-Adamite' world.	Some fossil men may have been found out of the 'correct' evolutionary sequence. Evolutionists must apply secondary explanations/assumptions to such finds.

PROBLEMS AND INCONSISTENCIES
SUMMARY

BIBLICAL	COMMENT
Noah's Flood — the only world-wide catastrophe that could be correlated with the fossil record.	Most of the fossil record is explained best on the basis of catastrophism.
The earth's being 'formless and void' was one of the early stages in the development of the earth.	Any catastrophe that left the earth 'formless and void' would have destroyed any geologic column or fossil record.
Romans 5:12 — There could not have been death of man or animal before Adam.	The origin or reason for death can be found only by revelation.
1 Corinthians 15:45 — The Bible clearly states that Adam was the FIRST man.	There is no evidence that man (although showing biological variation within limits) has ever been other than fully human.
As the Flood in Noah's day was sent as a judgment on mankind, it would appear logical that any fossil men in the fossil record would be of people living in Noah's day, or after (e.g. entombed in lesser catastrophes).	

with verse 2 containing three 'circumstantial clauses' — that is, three statements describing the circumstances attending what is described by the principal clause (v. 1). This conclusion is reinforced by the grammarian Gesenius who says that the conjunction *waw* ('and') at the beginning of verse 2 is a '*waw* copulative', which compares with the old English expression 'to wit'.

This grammatical connection between verses 1 and 2 rules out the 'gap' theory, because verse 2 is in fact a description of the state of the originally created earth. The New International Version (NIV) captures the sense: *'Now the earth was formless and empty . . .'*

'WAS' OR 'BECAME'?

'Gappists' translate verse 2 *'the earth **became** (or, had become) formless and empty'*, rather than *'the earth **was** formless and empty'*. At stake is the translation of the Hebrew word *hâyetah* (a form of the Hebrew verb, *hâyâh*, 'to be').

'Gap' theorist A. C. Custance claims that out of 1,320 occurrences of the verb *hâyâh* in the Old Testament, only 24 can certainly be said to bear the meaning 'to be'. He goes on to form the conclusion that in Genesis 1:2 *hâyetah* must mean 'became' and cannot mean simply 'was'.

Against this, we point out that the meaning or usage of a word is controlled by its context, and that the considerations raised in the previous section show that verse 2 is circumstantial to verse 1. Thus 'was' is the most natural and appropriate translation for *hâyetah*. It is rendered this way in most English versions (as well as in the LXX). This conclusion is supported by the fact that in Genesis 1:2 *hâyetah* is not followed by the preposition *le*, which would have removed any ambiguity and required the translation 'became'.

tôhû and *bôhû*

This delightful pair of words is usually translated 'formless and empty'; they imply that the original world was created unformed and unfilled and was, during six days, formed and filled by God's creative actions.

'Gappists' claim that these very words imply a process of judgmental destruction, and thus point to 'a sinful, and therefore, not an original state of the earth'. This relies upon importing into Genesis 1 interpretations found in other parts of the Old Testament (namely, Isaiah 34:11 and Jeremiah 4:23).

Tôhû and *bôhû* appear together in only the three above-mentioned places in the Old Testament, but *tôhû* appears alone in a number of others. In these, the simple meaning common to them all is 'formless'. The word itself does not tell us about the cause of formlessness; this has to be gleaned from the context. Isaiah 45:18 (often quoted by 'gappists') is rendered in the King James Version *'he created it not in vain [tôhû], he formed it to be inhabited.'* In the context, Isaiah is speaking about Israel, God's people, and His grace in restoring them. He did not choose His people in order to destroy them, but that He should be their God and they should be His people. Isaiah draws an analogy with God's purpose in creation: He did not create the world in order for it to be empty! No, He created it to be formed and filled, a suitable abode for His people. 'Gappists' are missing the point altogether when they argue that because Isaiah says God did not create the world *tôhû*, it must have become *tôhû* at some later time. Isaiah 45:18 is talking about God's **purpose** in creating, not about the original state of the creation.

Though the expressions *tôhû* and *bôhû* in both Isaiah 34:11 and Jeremiah 4:23 speak of a waste and emptiness resulting from divine judgment for sin, this meaning is not implicit in the expression itself, but is gained from the particular contexts in which it occurs. It is not valid therefore to infer and apply that meaning into Genesis 1:2, where the context does not require it.

The word 'replenish' in the King James translation of Genesis 1:28 did not mean 'restock' to the English readers of that day, but accurately reflected the original Hebrew, which means simply 'fill'. It cannot, therefore, be used to justify the idea that God's command meant them to REfill the earth.

CONCLUSION

The above discussion should serve to illustrate the very tenuous exegetical support which is used as argument for the 'gap' (or 'ruin-reconstruction') theory. Those who wish to pursue the details in greater depth should obtain and study the book *Unformed and Unfilled* by Weston W. Fields.

The simple, straightforward interpretation of Genesis 1:1–2 is that when God began creating the universe, the world was at first formless, empty, and dark, and God's Spirit hovered in powerful creative potential above the surging waters. It was through His creative energy that the world was progressively formed and filled during the subsequent six days.

FOOTNOTES

1. The most academic defence of the 'gap' theory is found in the book *Without Form and Void* by Arthur C. Custance (published by the author at Brookville, Canada, 1970). Currently, this 'ruin-reconstruction' view is held by many who use as Bible study aids the *Scofield Reference Bible or Dake's Annotated Reference Bible*. This view is also implied or allowed for in other Bibles such as *The Newberry Reference Bible*. *Dake's Annotated Reference Bible*, p. 51, states, '*When men finally agree on the age of the earth, then place the many years (over the historical 6,000) between Genesis 1:1 and 1:2, there will be no conflict between the Book of Genesis and Science*'.

2. *Unformed and Unfilled*. Weston W. Fields, Presbyterian & Reformed, Phillipsburg, New Jersey, 1976, p. 40.

3. *ibid.*, p. 7.

4. The term 'uniformitarian' refers to the idea that geological processes such as erosion, sedimentation, and earth movement have remained essentially the same throughout world history, and that 'the present is the key to the past'. But since the mid-nineteenth century the concept has been extended. According to Huxley, '*Consistent uniformitarianism postulates evolution as much in the organic as in the inorganic world.*' It is now assumed that a closed system exists, to which neither God nor any other non-human or non-natural force has access. (Quoted from *Man: Ape or Image*, J. Rendle-Short, Master Books, San Diego, 1984, p. 20, note 4).

5. For example, see Wysong, R., 1978, *The Creation-Evolution Controversy*, Inquiry Press, Midland, Michigan.

6. See Footnote 2.

10

Who was Cain's wife?

BEFORE answering this question, we need to consider nine major points recorded in the book of Genesis:

1. Adam was the first man (Genesis 2:7, 18–19 cf. 1 Corinthians 15:45).
2. Adam lived for 930 years (Genesis 5:5).
3. Eve was given that name because she was to be THE MOTHER OF ALL LIVING (Genesis 3:20).
4. Adam and Eve had MANY SONS AND DAUGHTERS (Genesis 5:4).
5. Everything was very good when first created (Genesis 1:31).
6. This goodness was marred when 'By one man sin entered the world' (Romans 5:12 cf. Genesis 3).
7. The creation was cursed by God (Genesis 3:17 cf. Romans 8:20–22) because of Adam's sin.
8. Abraham was married to his half-sister (Genesis 20:12).
9. The laws of incest had their origin only at the time of Moses (Leviticus 18–20).

These nine basic points provide clues that suggest Cain must have married his sister.

When God created Adam and Eve, they were the only human beings in existence. Genesis tells of the unique origin of each of them and how they were commanded to multiply and fill the earth (with their offspring).

Even though Adam and Eve had many sons and daughters, we are told the names of only three — Cain, Abel and Seth. These are spoken of in detail because of important events of which we need to be aware. What were these other children like? The Bible tells us that Adam and Eve's descendants went and built cities. For example, Cain went to the land of Nod with his wife and built a city (Genesis

115

4:16–17), constructed musical instruments (Genesis 4:21), and worked metals (Genesis 4:22).

So how does this tell us that Cain's wife was his sister? In Genesis 3:20 we read that Eve was given that name because she was to be the mother of **ALL** living — not just SOME of the living. Then Genesis 5:4 tells us that Adam and Eve had sons and daughters. Actually, Jewish tradition has it that they had 33 sons and 23 daughters![1] Don't forget — Adam did live for 930 years, so there was plenty of time! It is also clear from Scripture that Adam was the first man (1 Corinthians 15:45).

Putting all this together, the first two people, who were created by direct acts of God, had many children — sons and daughters. Obviously then, sons had to marry daughters for further generations to occur. Cain's wife had to be a very close relative!

Many people immediately reject this conclusion by appealing to the law of brother-sister incest. However, this law did not originate until the time of Moses (Leviticus 18–20). Remember that Abraham, who lived 400 years before Moses, was married to his half-sister. But how could this be so, especially in the light of the fact that brothers and sisters are not currently permitted by law to marry and to have children, because the offspring are likely to be deformed in some way? It is true that children produced as a result of a marriage between a brother and sister are likely to be deformed. As a matter of fact, the closer the couple are in relationship, the more likely it is that any offspring will be deformed. It is very easy for the layman to understand this without going into all the technical details. Each person inherits a set of genes from his or her mother and father. Unfortunately, these genes today contain many mistakes, and these mistakes show up in a variety of ways. For instance, some people let their hair grow over their ears to hide the fact that one ear is lower than the other, or perhaps someone's nose is not quite in the middle of his or her face; maybe someone's jaw is a little out of shape, and so on. Let's face it, the main reason we call each other 'normal' is because of our common agreement to do so!

Now the more closely related two people are, the more likely it is that they will have similar mistakes in their genes. Therefore brother and sister are likely to have similar mistakes in their genetic material. If there were to be a union between these two to produce offspring, then any child would inherit one set of genes from each of the parents. Because the genes probably have similar mistakes, the mistakes pair together and result in deformities in the children.

Conversely, the further away the parents are in relationship to each other, the more likely it is that they will have different mistakes in their genes. Children then, inheriting one set of genes from each parent, are likely to end up with some of the pairs of genes containing only one 'bad' gene in each pair. The 'good' gene then tends to overide the 'bad' so that a deformity (a serious one anyway) does not occur. Instead of having totally deformed ears for instance, a person may have only crooked ones!

But this fact of present-day life did not apply to Adam and Eve. When the first two people were created, they were perfect. Everything God made was 'very good' (Genesis 1:30). That means their genes were perfect. But, when sin entered the world (because of Adam) God cursed the world so that the perfect creation then began to degenerate, that is, suffer death and decay (Romans 1:22ff). Over a long period of time this degeneration would have resulted in all sorts of mistakes occurring in the genetic material of living things. Furthermore, such degeneration would have been particularly accelerated after the great Flood of Noah, due to the much harsher climatic conditions prevailing in the post-Flood world. For example, there would have been greater amounts of harmful, incoming cosmic radiation causing mutations (a technical term for accidents, damage and errors (e.g. copying mistakes) in the genes (hereditary information)). These mutations are passed on, after they occur, to the next generation and so they therefore accumulate with time in a population.

But Cain was the first child ever born. He would have received virtually no imperfect genes from Adam or Eve, and neither would any of Adam and Eve's

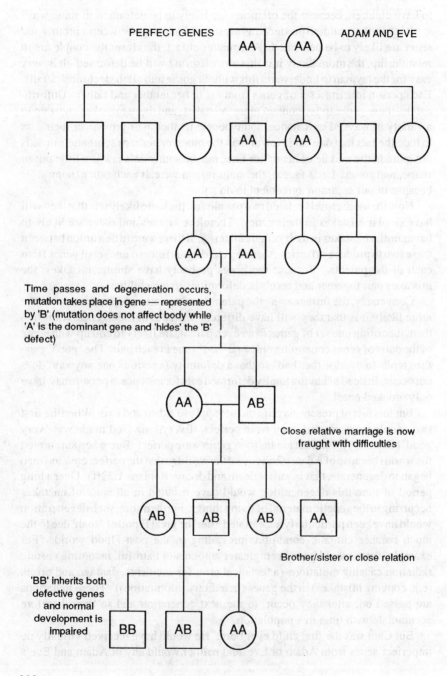

PERFECT GENES

AA — AA

ADAM AND EVE

AA   AA

AA — AA

AA — AA

Time passes and degeneration occurs, mutation takes place in gene — represented by 'B' (mutation does not affect body while 'A' is the dominant gene and 'hides' the 'B' defect)

AA — AB

Close relative marriage is now fraught with difficulties

AB — AB   AB   AA

Brother/sister or close relation

'BB' inherits both defective genes and normal development is impaired

BB   AB   AA

other children. In that situation brother and sister could have married without any potential to produce deformed offspring.

By the time of Moses (about 2,500 years later) degenerative mistakes would have accumulated to such an extent in the human race that it was necessary for God to bring in the laws of brother-sister (and close relative) incest (Leviticus 18–20). In all, there appear to be three inter-related reasons for the introduction of these laws:

1. As we have already discussed, there was the need to protect against the increasing potential to produce deformed offspring;
2. Apart from the obvious handicap that would be to all and sundry, these laws were instrumental in keeping the Jewish race strong, healthy, and within the purposes of God;
3. The laws were a means of protecting the individual, the family structure and society at large. The psychological damage caused by incestuous relationships cannot be minimized. One has only to look at our own society to recognize this fact.

Genesis is the record of the God Who was there as history happened. It is the Word of the One who knows everything, and who is a reliable Witness from the past. Thus, when we use Genesis as a basis for understanding history, we can make sense of evidence which would otherwise be a real mystery. You see, if evolution is true, science has an even bigger problem than Cain's wife to explain, namely how could man ever evolve by mutations in the first place, since that process on that basis would have made everyone's children deformed? The mere fact that even brothers and sisters can produce offspring which are still largely undeformed is a testimony to creation — not evolution.

FOOTNOTES

1. This figure is given in William Whiston's translation of *Josephus — Complete Works*, Antiquities III, 1, p. 27.

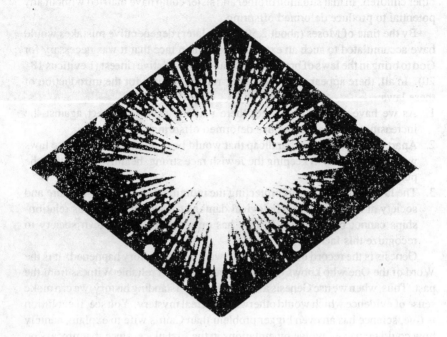

11

Doesn't distant starlight prove an old universe?

SOME stars are many millions of light-years away. Since a light-year is the distance travelled by light in one year, doesn't that mean that the universe is very old?

In spite of all the biblical and scientific evidence for a young earth/universe, this has long been a difficult problem. An explanation of origins which has scientific aspects must be capable of generating research, that is, it should have problems which need to be solved, and for years this has been one of them.

The assumptions behind the question seem rather commonsense, which makes it appear such a strong argument for long time-spans. In recent decades, however, the scientific community has been constrained by experiment and elegant mathematical proofs to accept many concepts as fact which common-sense would label as bizarre, especially in the fields of quantum mechanics and relativity. For example, whatever the mathematics may show, who could fully conceive of a concept such as curved space?

In this context it is interesting to note that a few years ago, two non-creationist researchers proposed that light from distant stars travelled through such curved space. Using their mathematics, it would take less than 20 years for light to get to us from stars billions of light-years away.[1] This idea is probably not correct, however, since it has been shown that it would mean we should see duplicates of everything.[2]

Perhaps the most commonly used explanation is that God created the light 'on its way', so that Adam could see the stars immediately without having to wait years for the light from even the closest stars to reach the earth. While we should not limit the power of God, this has some difficulties. It appears to imply that whenever we look at the behaviour of a very distant object, what we see happening never happened at all. To explain this, let's say we see an object a million light-years away which is exploding; that is, the light we receive in our telescopes carries this information 'recording' the explosion. When did that explosion take place? If the star that is exploding was created, say, only 6,000 years ago, then the explosion had to take place after that. Say it happened 5,000 years ago. Then the light from that explosion, if it is travelling constantly at today's speed, could not have reached the earth yet, because it would have covered a distance of only 5,000 light-years, a small fraction of the total distance of one million light-years. Yet we see the explosion in our telescopes. Does that mean it never happened?

Looked at another way, let's say that God created the light at the beginning extending all the way from the originally created star to the earth, say 6,000 years ago. That means that the light we are now receiving began its journey from a point along this light-path 6,000 light-years away from the earth, the point at which it

was created. Therefore this light which seems to show an exploding star never actually originated from an exploding star, and the information showing an explosion was created *en route* so to speak. It would thus appear that for such an explanation to hold true, for a 6,000-year-old universe, anything we see happening beyond about 6,000 light-years away is actually part of a gigantic picture-show of events which have not actually happened (deception?), showing us objects which may not even exist. This seems a major difficulty from many points of view.

A SOLUTION?

An obvious solution would be a higher speed of light in the past, allowing the light to cover the same distance more quickly. But why, and when, was this high-speed light switched into 'low gear'? Whether true or not, this seems at first glance a too-convenient *ad hoc* explanation.

However, an Australian (Barry Setterfield) has raised this possibility in a fascinating way. His interest had been aroused by discovering that around the 1930s, there was a controversy in the scientific literature: astronomer Gheury de Bray had pointed out a persistent tendency for successive measurements of the speed of light to be less than before. Was the speed of light decreasing? If so, this could indicate that it was much faster in the past, and would point the way to a solution for the problem being discussed here.

Setterfield and his later co-worker, Trevor Norman of the Mathematics Department of Flinders University, South Australia, collected all the measurements that had been made on the speed of light (which is usually abbreviated with the symbol c). Over the past 300 years c has been measured many times, using various methods, such as the eclipse of Jupiter's moons. This method, using vast distances which we now know accurately, enabled the early measurements to be done with quite reasonable precision, even using early clocks with an accuracy of only one or two seconds. Not only did there appear to be a trend for c to decrease, but it appeared that the rate of change was higher in the early years of measurements. This rate of change decreased progressively until by 1960 it seemed to have become zero, that is, c appeared to be fairly constant after that date. This suggested that a logarithmic or geometric expression (a complex mathematical equation) was the best way to describe the behaviour of c. Norman

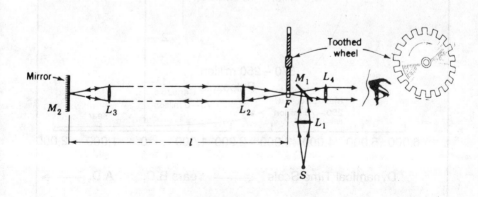

An apparatus for measuring the speed of light. It was designed by nineteenth century French physicist Hippolyte Louis Fizeau.

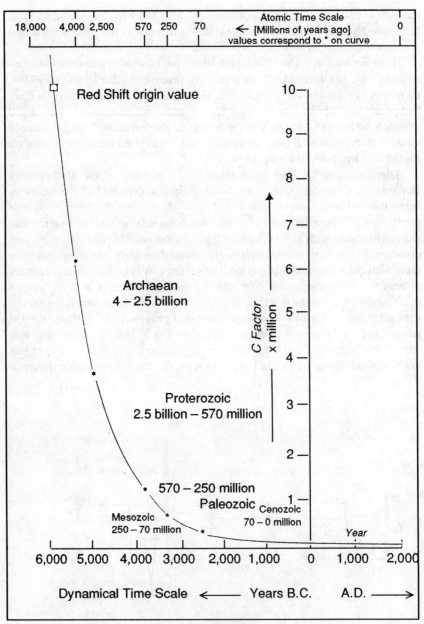

C Decay in Dynamical Time

Fig. 1

and Setterfield maintain that only a handful of mathematical curves fit the observational data points well.

For instance, the curve in Figure 1 shows that c was nearly infinite just a few thousand years ago, which means that light could reach us from the most distant parts of the universe well within the Genesis time-scale. If true, it would mean that observing light today is like watching a jumbo jet taxiing slowly to its hangar, having travelled most of its journey at a previously much faster speed before slowing down.

At this point it should be noted that a higher c in the past would have a lot of fascinating and very important 'spin-offs'. For instance, if c was higher, atomic processes which are linked to c mathematically would also have been faster, including all forms of radioactive decay. The billions of years of earth history assumed by radioactive dating advocates would collapse into a few thousand. This argument is why this concept deserves very careful attention.

A SCIENTIFIC CONTROVERSY

However, there is currently considerable controversy in creationist circles about the validity of the statistical methods used to demonstrate the decline, with qualified statisticians able to be found to support both viewpoints with equal fervour. If the controversy is resolved in favour of the idea that the historical data, while not denying it, cannot be used to give statistical support to the idea of declining c, there still remains an apparent trend which requires explanation. (One would expect *random* errors to give readings both *above* and *below* the true value of c.)

So far, the best explanation put forward by the critics for this apparent downward trend is a psychological effect. They suggest that each researcher may have been biased against publishing a result which differed too much from results published previously. Thus, according to this explanation, if the first result was too high, subsequent ones will gradually head towards the correct value. This seems a rather difficult idea to test with any certainty, and it is not born out in other issues, where as a rule scientists have had no hesitation in trying to prove their rivals wrong.

MORE EVIDENCE?

The evidence gathered by Norman and Setterfield in their monograph[3] (currently in the process of revision) extends beyond the measurements themselves. Much of it could be called secondary evidence resulting from the predicted consequences of such a drop in c. For instance, the various atomic constants (e.g.

Planck's constant) generally have c terms in the equations which describe them. In some, the c terms cancel out. Therefore, in some instances, a decreasing c should give rise to decreasing values for that particular constant; in others an increasing trend should be apparent; in still others no trend (the c terms cancel out). The data presented by these authors for 13 such constants shows confirmation of the expected trend in each case, at least by visual inspection. Unfortunately, for most of the constants, only a few measurements are available, especially for earlier years. Another potential problem arises in that it is not yet clear whether, in at least some cases, the reported value of the constant has been calculated from the values of c accepted at the time. In which case any trend could not be regarded as independent confirmation.

Another predicted result of c decline is that atomic time should be slowing down relative to dynamic (gravitational) time — for example, as measured by the moon's orbit. The authors cite a long series of observations, from 1955 to 1981, by a respected scientist (van Flandern) who has compared the two 'clocks' and shown that they are indeed changing relative to each other (that is, atomic clocks are slowing down or gravitational clocks are speeding up). Some have tried to explain the discrepancy by suggesting that the gravitational constant G may be changing. This is, however, unconfirmed, and the fact remains that if atomic clocks have indeed been slowing with time, this is, *prima facie*, a confirmation of a prediction of the Norman–Setterfield model. To make things even more confusing, some literature challenges have arisen in regard to the van Flandern measurements. Attempts to contact the scientist himself have been unsuccessful.

SOME OBJECTIONS

One objection says that by the Einstein equation $E=mc^2$, if c is a million times faster, then the energy, especially of atomic reactions, should be a million million times higher.

This objection was answered in the early stages of the c decay research. There have been counter-objections, and counter-counter objections. The Norman–Setterfield work has convinced some substantially qualified people, and antagonized many more. It is clearly an emotionally charged issue, and an enormously complex one which requires expertise in more fields than are usually found in any one individual. At the time of writing, a new upgraded version of their monograph is in preparation, we are informed, with a third co-author.

The objection that Adam would have fried from the early radioactive heating has also been addressed. There has been an ongoing exchange about reworked values of the early c measurements, apparent selectivity of data, as well as various astronomical objections, several of which have appeared in creationist literature. Other more esoteric objections have recently been raised and it is important that all of these be dealt with in their ongoing research. The issue is too important to ignore, and its enormous complexity ensures that qualified people will still be arguing back and forth for many years before the matter is fully resolved.

CONTRIBUTION FROM AN UNEXPECTED QUARTER

In 1987 an article appeared in a respected astrophysical journal by the Russian astrophysicist, Professor Troitskii[4]. Though an evolutionist, he is convinced that the best cosmological model relative to the available astronomical data is a universe beginning with an infinite speed of light, declining to its present level. While Troitskii doesn't even mention any actual measurements of c, his contribution is certainly pertinent, especially in considering claims that a declining c would contradict basic principles of physics. It certainly shows that, no matter what the outcome, it is not simply a case of 'creationists bending the laws of science to suit themselves' as has been suggested.

FURTHER CONSEQUENCES

If c has declined in the past, the following may also be true.
● **Red-shift**
Light reaching us from stars that are more distant would then have 'slowed down' more (relative to its initial speed compared with light from closer stars). It has been stated that this would mean that it would carry a built-in 'red-shift' (that is, its frequency shifted to the red end of the spectrum) such that light from

the most distant stars would be the most red-shifted.

This is in fact what is observed. The most obvious and widely held explanation for this observation (progessively increasing red-shift) has been that it is a 'Doppler' effect (like the changing frequency of a train-whistle depending on whether it is approaching us or going away from us). The 'big bang' explanation that is currently popular would claim that the most distant stars are also those with the fastest speed, hence they have the biggest red-shift. More than one non-creationist astronomer (e.g. Halton Arp) has claimed that the red-shifts we observe cannot all be explained as Doppler effects anyway. If the red-shift is not a Doppler effect but is due to a decrease in c, it could mean that the universe is not, after all, expanding, and may even be contracting.

● **Microwave background**

There is a 'background' of radiation coming from all parts of space, equivalent to a black body radiat-
ing at a temperature of
about three degrees
Kelvin. This has been
interpreted as the 'left-
over echo' of the
imagined cosmic fire-
ball. However, if the c-
decline/red-shift ex-
planation is correct, it
would also appear to
predict such a back-
ground, this time from
the massive red-shift-
ing of the light from
the most distant ob-

jects, closest to the time of creation. In fact, the energy density of this radiation has been shown to be consistent with red-shifted starlight.

There are other interesting explanations suggested by c decay, ranging from rapid past nuclear processes in stars (hence their rapid 'stellar evolution' — actually 'degeneration' is a better word) to the nature of quasars. The interested reader is advised to watch Creation Science Foundation literature for any updates on the controversy.[5]

COULD IT BE DISPROVED?

As mentioned earlier, it may turn out that the historical measurements cannot be used as statistical evidence for c decline. That would not, of course, show that c had not declined in exactly the way suggested by the authors. The concept could be falsified, perhaps, by bringing up an unanswerable objection (that is, if c is faster, such and such is the consequence, which is impossible . . .). However, we need to be cautious here, because this may reflect our ignorance. Some of the 'unanswerable' objections brought against c decline in the 1930s have since been shown to be based on a lack of understanding of atomic physics which has since advanced considerably.

POSSIBLE EXPERIMENTAL PROOF?

If c has been declining, it is possible that the reason it appeared to cease its drop in 1960 may turn out to be that virtually all measurements made after that date were done using atomic clocks. These would be changing in concert with c so as to make any change undetectable, even if it is occurring. It may be possible to detect a change in c happening in the next few years using appropriate methods. In fact, according to one of the suggested mathematical curves, c may even begin to increase after reaching a minimum.

WHAT IF FURTHER RESEARCH INVALIDATES THE IDEA THAT *C* HAS CHANGED IN THE PAST FEW CENTURIES?

This may well turn out to be the case, in spite of the fact that it would leave one wondering why all the seemingly tantalizing coincidences all pointed in that direction initially. It may turn out to be an issue in which ultimate proof or disproof remains for ever out of reach (unless c is still declining, as discussed above). However, the researchers will still have done an enormous service. The large

amount of theoretical work they have undertaken on the consequences of c changing has made many realize that the idea of c beginning at a near-infinite speed and declining to its present value encounters fewer objections than at first imagined. In addition, supported unintentionally by the evolutionist Troitskii, they have shown that such a concept (even if it happened well **before** anyone began to measure c), may make for a more consistent cosmological model than the 'big bang'.

It will also have been a fascinating example of the limitations of science when it comes to interpreting the past from present evidence. In this case, it has shown

how one piece of information not hitherto suspected could have profound and far-reaching effects in our interpretation of events which were previously thought to be established with certainty. To explain further. IF in fact c had declined from a near-infinite beginning point to a zero rate of change (there are many such mathematical decay processes in nature), whether recently or hundreds of years before man began to measure, the following would automatically be the case:

- Starlight would be on the earth from virtually the moment the first stars were created.
- There would be no need to postulate billions of years for light to reach us from very distant objects.
- Radiometric dating results given as billions of years should, in fact, be interpreted as thousands of years of faster decay when c was higher.
- The progressive red-shift of stars, as well as the cosmic microwave background, may in fact be a consequence of declining c, rather than the result of universal expansion from an original 'big bang'.

And yet, a modern-day scientist, ignorant of a previous change in c, would still feel justified in clinging to all the old theories as if they were as well established as the law of gravity.

We can see that humility is very much in order. It has happened over and over that the majority of archaeologists, for instance, were adamant that things stated very clearly in the Bible were wrong and contrary to scientific evidence. In each case, further information came to light which showed that the Bible was right after all. We do not know everything — no scientist will ever know everything. Evolutionists have repeatedly made dogmatic statements of certainty about the past which have later led to embarrassment. Creation scientists should try to avoid similar dogmatism about matters on which Scripture is silent.

We may never know with scientific certainty exactly how God created a cosmos which is both extremely large and relatively young. The c change proposal shows, however, that it is not necessary to postulate a whole string of miraculous *ad hoc* suspensions of natural law to explain data which appears to be contrary to a young universe.

The reader would do well to remember that scientific theories in all areas, no matter how convincing, may be replaced by others as new evidence comes to hand (this includes creationist as well as evolutionist theories). In contrast, the Word of the One who alone has access to all the evidence is an 'everlasting rock'. Research based on assumptions which are in opposition to these revealed truths will lead to conclusions which will inevitably turn out to be erroneous.

REFERENCES

1. Moon, P. and Spencer, D. T., 1953. Binary stars and the velocity of light. *Journal of the Optical Society of America*, vol. 43(8), pp. 635–641.
2. Bounds, V., 1984. Towards a critical examination of the historical basis of the idea that light has slowed down. *Ex Nihilo Technical Journal*, vol. 1, pp. 105–117.
3. Norman T. and Setterfield, B., 1987. *The Atomic Constants, Light and Time*. Flinders University of South Australia School of Mathematical Sciences. Technical Report prepared for: Lambert T. Dolphin, who was at that time Senior Research Physicist, Geoscience and Engineering Centre, Stanford Research Institute International.
4. Troitskii, V. S., 1987. Physical constants and evolution of the universe. *Astrophysics and Space Science*, vol. 139, pp. 389–411.
5. For example, see *Creation* magazine, Vol. 12 No. 3, June–August, 1990, pp. 40–41.

STOP PRESS

At the time of final preparation of this article, one of us (Dr Carl Wieland) received a telephone call from Dr Michael Hasofer, who is Professor of Statistics at the University of New South Wales in Sydney, Australia. He had been asked to give an impartial assessment on the controversy about the statistical methods used. (A substantial body of opinion has claimed that when the more appropriate weighted methods are used, there is no statistical evidence of changing c.) We had previously understood from Professor Hasofer that he agreed with the use of weighted data, but that to be fair, fitting them to a straight line was not an appropriate test of the hypothesis. On this telephone call, he stated that he had found that using a 'weighted regression' to fit the data to a particular curve gave a 'highly significant' result in favour of changing *c*. His technical report appears in Volume 4 of the *Ex Nihilo Technical Journal*, produced by Creation Science Foundation.

12

How did various animals get from the Ark to isolated places such as Australia?

THERE is no doubt that the whole issue of post-Flood animal migration patterns presents some tough problems and research challenges to the biblical creation model. There are severe practical limitations on our attempts to understand the hows and whys of something which happened once, was not recorded in detail, and cannot be repeated.

Let's begin by reaffirming that God's Word does indeed reveal, in the plainest possible terms, that the whole globe was inundated with a violent, watery cataclysm. The only survivors were the inhabitants of the Ark, which included at least one breeding pair of every kind of land-dwelling, air-breathing creature.

Any difficulties in our ability to explain every single situation in detail must therefore be a reflection of our limited understanding. When Krakatoa erupted in 1883, the island remnant remained lifeless for some years, but was eventually colonized by a surprising variety of creatures, including not only insects and earthworms, but birds, lizards, snakes and even a few mammals. One would not have expected some of this surprising array of creatures to have been able to cross the ocean as they obviously did. Even though these were in the main smaller than some of the creatures we will discuss here, it usefully illustrates the limits of our *a priori* imaginings on such things.

For the most part, the animals of Noah's day were faced with far fewer such apparently insuperable difficulties. The Ararat region is more or less the mathematical centre of the earth's land-masses.[1]

Evolutionary anthropologists themselves have no difficulty in acknowledging that men and animals were once freely able to cross the Bering Strait, which separates Asia and the Americas. In fact, before the idea of continental drift became popular, evolutionists taught and believed that a lowering of the sea level during an ice age (with more water locked up at the poles) would mean that there were land bridges enabling dry-land passage from Europe most of the way to Australasia, for example.

The existence of some deep-water stretches along this route is consistent with this explanation; evolutionist geologists themselves believe there have been major tectonic upheavals, accompanied by substantial rising and falling of sea-floors, in the time-period which they themselves associate with an ice age. For instance, parts of California are believed to have been raised many thousands of feet from what was the sea-floor during this ice age period,[2] which they term 'Pleistocene' (one of the most recent of the supposed geological time periods); in the same way other dry-land areas, including parts of these land bridges, fell to become submerged at around the same time. Most Pleistocene sediments are regarded by creationist geologists as post-Flood, the period in which these major migrations would have taken place.

There is a widespread, but mistaken, belief that marsupials are found only in Australia, thus supporting the idea that they must have evolved here. Live

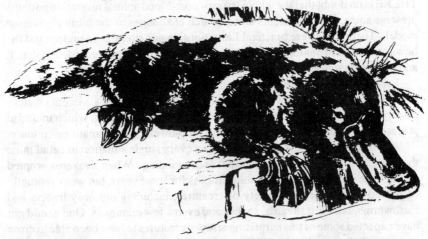

marsupials are found also in America, for instance, and fossil marsupials even in Europe. Therefore, in evolutionary terms, since they are all believed to have come from a common ancestor, migration between Australia and other areas must have been possible.

Creationists generally believe there was one great Ice Age after, and as a consequence of, the Flood.[3] This made it possible for animals to migrate over land-bridges for centuries. Those creationists who do accept some form of continental break-up after the Flood[4] often believe this to have been in the 'days of Peleg'. This again would mean several centuries for animals to disperse, in this instance without the necessity of land-bridges.

How did animals make the long journey? Even though there have been isolated reports of individual animals making startling journeys of thousands of miles, such abilities are not even necessary. A very small number of rabbits were released in Australia by early settlers. Wild rabbits are now found at the very opposite corner (in fact, every corner) of this vast continent. Does that mean that an individual rabbit had to be capable of crossing the whole of Australia? Of course not. Creation speakers are often asked mockingly 'Did the kangaroo hop all the way to Australia?' but we see by the rabbit example that this is a somewhat foolish question. However, let us answer it, anyway.

DID THE KANGAROO HOP ALL THE WAY TO AUSTRALIA?

Populations of animals may have had centuries to migrate, relatively slowly, over many generations.

Incidentally, the opposite question (also common), as to whether the two kangaroos hopped all the way **from** Australia to the Ark, is also easily answered. The continents we now have, with their load of Flood-deposited sedimentary rock, are not the same as whatever continents there may have been in the pre-Flood world. We also have **no** information as to how animals were distributed. Kangaroos (as

is true for any other creature) may not have been on any isolated land-mass. In fact, Genesis 1:9 suggests that there may have been only one land-mass. (*'Let the waters under the heavens be gathered together into one place, and let the dry **land** appear.'*) For all we know, kangaroos might have been feeding within a stone's throw of Noah while he was building the Ark.

It may be asked, if creatures were migrating to Australia over a long time (which journey would have included such places as Indonesia, presumably) why do we not find their fossils *en route* in such countries? But fossilization is a rare event, requiring, as a rule, sudden burial to prevent decomposition. Lions lived in Palestine until relatively recent times. Not surprisingly, we don't find lion fossils in Palestine, yet this doesn't prevent us believing the many historical

Fig. 1

reports of their presence. The millions of bison that once roamed the United States of America have left virtually no fossils. So why should it be a surprise that small populations, presumably under migration pressure from competitors and/or predators and thus living in only one area for a few generations at most, should leave no fossils?

Another issue is the question of why certain animals (and plants) are uniquely found in only one place. Why is species 'x' found only in Madagascar? And species 'y' only in the Seychelles? Many times questions on this are phrased to indicate that the questioner believes that this means that species 'y' headed only in that one direction, and never migrated anywhere else. But this is not so, of course. All that the present situation indicates is that these are now the only places where 'x' or 'y' **still survive**.

The ancestors of present-day kangaroos may have established daughter populations in different parts of the world which subsequently became extinct. Perhaps only those marsupials that reached Australia ahead of the placental mammals (we are not suggesting anything other than random processes in choice of destination), to be subsequently isolated from most of the latter, have been able to survive and prosper.

Palm Valley in Central Australia is host to a unique species of palms, *Livingstonia mariae*, found nowhere else in the world (see Figure 1). Does this necessarily mean that the seeds for this species floated only to this one little spot? Not at all. Current models of post-Flood climate indicate that the world is much drier now than it was in the early post-Flood centuries. Evolutionists themselves agree that in recent times (by evolutionary standards), the Sahara was lush and green, and Central Australia had a moist, tropical climate. For all we know, the *Livingstonia mariae* palm may have been widespread over much of Australia — perhaps even in other places which are now dry, such as parts of Africa.

The palm has survived in Palm Valley because there it happens to be protected from the drying out which affected the rest of its vast Centralian surrounds. Everywhere else, it happened to die out.

Incidentally, this concept of changing vegetation with changing climate should be kept in mind when considering post-Flood animal migration. Especially because of the objections (and caricatures) which may be presented. For instance, how could creatures that today need a rainforest environment trudge across millions of acres of parched desert on the way to where they now live? The answer is that the desert simply wasn't desert!

THE KOALA AND OTHER SPECIALIZED TYPES

Some problems are more difficult to solve. For instance, there are creatures that require special conditions or a very specialized diet, such as the giant panda of China or Australia's koala. We don't know, of course, that bamboo shoots or blue gum leaves[5] were not then flourishing all along their eventual respective migratory paths. In fact, this may have influenced the direction they took.

But in any case, there is another possibility. Specialization, in the sense of a need for unique or special conditions to survive, may be a downhill change in some populations. That is, it may result from a loss in genetic information from thinning out of the gene pool or by degenerative mutation. A good example is the fact that many modern breeds of dog, selected by man (although natural conditions can do likewise), are much less hardy in the wild than their mongrel ancestors. The St Bernard carries a mutational defect (thyroid overproduction) which means it needs special conditions (icy cold) to prevent overheating.

The suggestion here is that the ancestors of these creatures, when they came

. . . the possibility of transport by large floating masses of matted vegetation or even by logs serving as rafts . . .

off the Ark, were not as specialized and thus were more hardy than their descendants, who carry only a portion of that original gene pool of information.[6] In other words, the koala's ancestor may have been able to survive on a much greater range of vegetation. Such an explanation has been made possible only with modern biological insights; perhaps as knowledge increases, some of the remaining difficulties will become less so.[7]

The sloth, a very slow-moving creature, may seem to require much more time than Scripture allows to make the journey from Ararat to its present home. Ignoring the possibility of transport by large floating masses of matted vegetation, perhaps its present condition is also explicable by a similar 'devolutionary' process.

Such changes do not require large time periods for animals under migratory pressure; the first small population that forms would tend to break up rapidly into daughter populations, going in different directions, each carrying only a portion of the gene pool of the original pair that came off the Ark.

Sometimes all of a population will eventually become extinct, sometimes all but one specialized type. Where all the sub-types survive and proliferate, there is found some of the tremendous diversity seen among some groups of creatures which are apparently derived from one created kind. This explains why some very obviously related species are found far apart from each other.

We may never know the exact answer to every one of such questions, but certainly one can see that the problems are far less formidable than they may at first appear.[8] Coupled with all the biblical, geological and anthropological evidence for Noah's Flood, one is justified in regarding the Genesis account of the animals' dispersing from a central point as perfectly reasonable in principle and in broad outline.[9]

FOOTNOTES

1. Woods, Andrew J., 1973. *The centre of the earth*, ICR Technical Monograph No. 3.
2. Dr Steven Austin, Institute for Creation Research, San Diego, USA, personal communication.
3. See 'Were there really ice ages?', this volume, pp. 51–57.
4. See 'What about continental drift?', this volume, pp. 27–40.
5. Actually, the koala can eat other types of gum leaves. Australia has around 500 species of eucalypt (gum) trees. Koalas eat the leaves of about 20 species, with the blue gum certainly a favourite. Also, the giant panda which usually only eats bamboo shoots, has been known to eat small animals on occasion.
6. See 'How did all the different races arise (from Noah's family)?', this volume, pp. 85–100, for an example of the way in which a very light-skinned race springing from a mid-brown one is missing some of the information in its parent population.
7. A detailed study of genetic changes in post-Flood migrating primates and the fossils along their migration routes can be read in *Ex Nihilo Technical Journal*, Vol. 4, (1990), pp. 5–53. (Available from Creation Science Foundation.)
8. In recent literature considering some of the vexing problems of animal distribution even within an evolutionary framework, there has been an occasional refocusing of emphasis on the fact that early man may have been a much better boat-builder and navigator than previously thought. Various types of animals may thus have crossed the sea, accompanying man. This should be kept in mind as a possibility in a few instances. Animals brought in this way to a new continent may have prospered, even though the accompanying humans returned or eventually perished.
9. For further reading: *The Genesis Flood*, Whitcomb, J. and Morris, H. Presbyterian and Refer-formed, Phillipsburg, New Jersey, 1961.

The family magazine on creation

CREATION
magazine

Become enthralled as your family journeys into a world of scientific discoveries that show God's greatness; of nature articles that reveal the wonders of God's creation; of biblical accounts that show God's Word is true; of ideas that have shaken the world; of great scientists who have devoted their lives to revealing some of God's creation through their work.

The evidence for God's creation and the good news about the Creator, Jesus Christ, are a joy for us to share. *We'd love you to share our enthusiasm.*

Why not join our readers from around the world who eagerly await each quarterly issue? *Creation* magazine helps you counteract evolution's damaging influences while showing the relevance of creation to your daily life.

Write today so we can send your first exciting issue!